The PILGRIM'S *Journal*

WELLSPRING
North Palm Beach, Florida

Published by Wellspring

Design by Ashley Wirfel
Cover Illustration by Ben Skudlarek

ISBN: 978-1-63582-098-0 (softcover)
ISBN: 978-1-63582-137-6 (eBook)

10 9 8 7 6 5 4 3 2 1

Printed in the United States of America

Table of Contents

Introduction

Are You a *Pilgrim* or a *Tourist?*

My good friend, Father Bob, and I have been hosting pilgrimages for a long, long time. Our current schedule includes three trips each year: the Holy Land; Lourdes and Paris, in France; and Rome, Assisi, and Florence, in Italy. On the opening night as we welcome the pilgrims, we always ask them the same question: Are you going to be a pilgrim or are you going to be a tourist?

Tourists want everything to go exactly as they have planned and imagined it. They rush around from one place to another making sure they cram everything in. They are constantly buying souvenirs and knickknacks, many of which they will look at when they get home and wonder, "What was I thinking?" Tourists get upset if there are delays. They demand prompt attention and service to their every need and desire. They focus on themselves, often shoving past others to get where they want to go. Tourists go sightseeing. Tourists count the cost.

Pilgrims are very different. They look for signs. If a flight gets delayed or canceled, they ask, "What is God trying to say to me?" Pilgrims are not concerned with seeing and doing everything, just the things they feel called to see and do. They are not obsessed with shopping. They are aware of the needs of others. Pilgrims go looking for meaning. Pilgrims count their blessings.

The reality is we are all pilgrims. This planet we call earth is not our home; we are just passing through. We build homes and establish ourselves here on earth in ways that ignore that we are really just here for a short time. It is a dangerous pastime to live as if you were never going to die, but consciously or subconsciously we all fall into this trap to various degrees.

We are only here on earth for the blink of an eye. This is not our home. That's why the happiness that God wants and created us for is very different from the fleeting happiness and momentary pleasures of this world. God created us for lasting happiness in a changing world and eternal happiness with him in heaven. The happiness he wants for us in this life is a rare kind of happiness that is not dependent on situations or circumstances. It is easy to be happy when everything is going well. But Christian joy allows us to be happy like Paul was when he was in prison.

Do you ever think about heaven? It seems to me we don't talk about it anywhere near as much as we should. When Rudyard Kipling was very seriously ill a nurse asked him, "Is there anything you want?" He replied, "I want God!" We all do. We may not be aware of it, but we want God. Behind every desire for a new car or a new house, a promotion or accomplishment, clothes and jewelry, plastic surgery, adventure and travel, food and sex, acceptance and comfort, is our desire for God. We are always hungry for something more complete, and God is that completeness that we yearn for from the depths of our soul.

We are just passing through, and it is helpful to remind ourselves of that from time to time. In the context of eternity, we are only here for the blink of an eye. Realizing this changes our priorities. At the same time, we are here for a reason. You are here for a reason. God has a mission for you.

Life is a pilgrimage, a sacred journey. Typically, it is a journey to a shrine or other location important to a person's faith or beliefs. You can make a pilgrimage to the Holy Land, Rome, Fatima, Lourdes, the Camino, or any of the famous Catholic sites around the world. But you could also make a pilgrimage to your nearest Cathedral. In fact, every Sunday you make a pilgrimage to your local parish to Mass.

Very often people make pilgrimages with special intentions in mind. Some ask God for a favor, perhaps to heal a loved one who is sick. Others make a pilgrimage in thanksgiving for a blessing they have already received from God. There are always couples on your trips who are celebrating a wedding anniversary. They are making the trip to thank God for their marriage. On every trip, Father Bob chooses one of the holy places and invites every couple on the trip to renew their marriage vows. Powerful! I cannot even describe how powerful and moving this is. I have seen it many times, but still it moves me. Sometimes people make a pilgrimage seeking clarity on some decision they have to make.

Life is a pilgrimage, but sometimes you need a pilgrimage to discover life. We are journeying in this life toward the sacred city, toward the heart of God—heaven. Nobody makes the journey alone. We all need companions. Some of my very best friends in this world I met on pilgrimages. These trips that Dynamic Catholic hosts are life changing, and when you experience something like that with other people, you form a very special bond.

The best friends in the world encourage us and challenge us to become the-vest-version-of-ourselves, and by doing so, they help us to get to heaven.

Let us pray for the grace to be pilgrims and not just tourists. Let us pray for the grace to be the kind of friend who helps others in the great pilgrimage of life.

This is "A Pilgrim's Prayer," by Thomas Merton:

> My Lord God,
> I have no idea where I am going.
> I do not see the road ahead of me.
> I cannot know for certain where it will end. . . .
> Nor do I really know myself,
> And the fact that I think I am following Your will
> Does not mean that I am actually doing so.
> But I believe that the desire to please You does in fact please You.
> And I hope I have that desire in all that I am doing.
> I hope that I will never do anything apart from that desire.
> And I know that if I do this,
> You will lead me by the right road, though I may know nothing about it.
> Therefore will I trust You always though I may seem lost
> And in the shadow of death.
> I will not fear, for You are ever with me,
> And You will never leave me to face my perils alone.

We are just passing through this place we call earth. At every turn we are tempted to be tourists, but we are pilgrims. Spend some time today thinking about heaven.

Pilgrim's Prayer

Beloved *Jesus*, we are Your pilgrims, and are on our way to You. Anoint us to do Your will as we travel on this journey. Help us to be grateful for this opportunity to travel through the foreign lands. Help us give a hand of friendship and love to fellow pilgrims. May the joy of Your dwelling in us draw us closer to each other and to You.

Give us strength to persevere when we get too tired. Give us understanding of different nationalities, cultures, wealth, poverty, and mentalities. Give us patience and grace to accept diversity in the food, services, and people we encounter.

Remind us to offer gratitude to our hosts, tour guides, and hotel and airline personnel, and to offer them forgiveness when needed. Expand our vision to recognize Your plan. Warm our hearts by the flame of Your love, so that we may share it with others too. Open our lips so that we can speak Your Word and words of love.

Expand our arms so that we can embrace each other and all who need hugs. Speak to us so that we may discern the role that You have for us. Send us a breeze when it gets too hot, or sunshine when it's raining too hard.

Help us to love, pray, forgive, embrace, see, and discover. Help us to remember: We responded to Your calling to make this journey. We are Your pilgrims, going towards

You and for You. If we feel lonely, we will remember that we are not alone as with each step we take, You are right alongside us. And if at times the road is too rocky, if the weather gets too stormy, if it gets dark, if our hearts grow numb, heavy, empty, shivering, broken, then, especially then, help us to remember how much You love us.

We promise to remember that You hold our souls. And always, God, help us to live according to Your will.

Amen.

- *By Milanka Lachman,*
Founder & President, 206 Tours

Journal Pages

The following pages are blank for you to spend some time journaling before you leave, while you are on pilgrimage, and when you return. It's amazing what we think we will remember that we ultimately forget. This will become a keepsake in the years for you to come, a place you can return to relive the memories, the spiritual experiences, and to see how much you have grown.

What are your hopes for this journey?

What is God saying to you today?

What are your hopes for this journey?

What is God saying to you today?

Day One

What is God saying to you today?

What do you want to remember about today?

What is God saying to you today?

What do you want to remember about today?

Day Three

What is God saying to you today?

What do you want to remember about today?

Day Four

What is God saying to you today?

What do you want to remember about today?

Day Five

What is God saying to you today?

What do you want to remember about today?

Day Six

What is God saying to you today?

What do you want to remember about today?

Day Seven

What is God saying to you today?

What do you want to remember about today?

Day Eight

What is God saying to you today?

What do you want to remember about today?

Day Nine

What is God saying to you today?

What do you want to remember about today?

Day Ten

What is God saying to you today?

What do you want to remember about today?

Day Eleven

What is God saying to you today?

What do you want to remember about today?

Day Twelve

What is God saying to you today?

What do you want to remember about today?

**If your pilgrimage is longer than 12 days,
continue your journaling on the notes pages at the end of the journal.*

What is God saying to you today?

How did your pilgrimage inspire you?

What is God saying to you today?

How does your pilgrimage continue to inspire you?

What is God saying to you today?

How does your pilgrimage continue to inspire you?

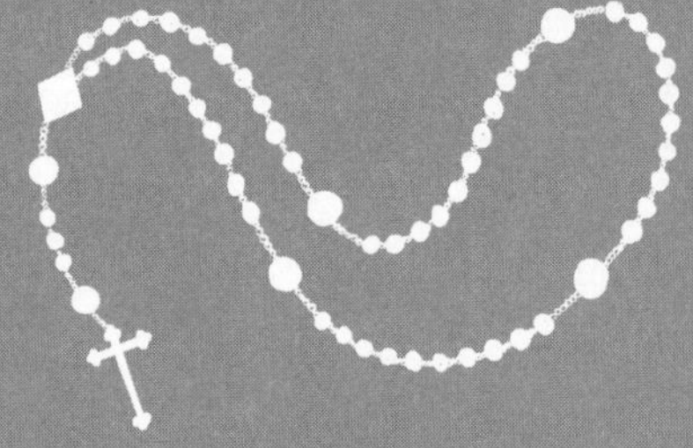

The Holy Rosary

The *Four Things* You Need to Know to Pray the Rosary:

1. The prayers
2. The mysteries
3. The rosary beads
4. How the beads are used

The Prayers of the Rosary

The Sign of the Cross
In the name of the Father, and of the Son, and of the Holy Spirit. Amen

The Apostles' Creed
I believe in God, the Father almighty, Creator of heaven and earth, and in Jesus Christ, his only Son, our Lord, who was conceived by the Holy Spirit, born of the Virgin Mary, suffered under Pontius Pilate, was crucified, died, and was buried; he descended into hell; on the third day he rose again from the dead; he ascended into heaven, and is seated at the right hand of God the Father almighty; from there he will come to judge the living and the dead. I believe in the Holy Spirit, the holy catholic Church, the communion of saints, the forgiveness of sins, the resurrection of the body, and life everlasting. Amen.

Our Father

Our Father, who art in heaven, hallowed be thy name. Thy kingdom come, thy will be done on earth as it is in heaven. Give us this day our daily bread, and forgive us our trespasses, as we forgive those who trespass against us. And lead us not into temptation, but deliver us from evil. Amen.

Hail Mary

Hail Mary, full of grace, the Lord is with thee. Blessed art thou among women, and blessed is the fruit of thy womb, Jesus. Holy Mary, mother of God, pray for us sinners, now and at the hour of our death. Amen. Glory Be Glory be to the Father, and to the Son, and to the Holy Spirit, as it was in the beginning, is now and ever shall be, world without end. Amen.

*The Fatima Prayer**

O my Jesus, forgive us our sins, save us from the fires of hell. Lead all souls to heaven, especially those in most need of thy mercy.

**This is the prayer that was added in the early twentieth century in response to the vision of Fatima; it is an optional addition to the Rosary.*

Hail Holy Queen

Hail Holy Queen, Mother of mercy, our life, our sweetness, and our hope. To thee do we cry, poor banished children of Eve. To thee do we send up our sighs, mourning and weeping in this valley of tears. Turn then, most gracious Advocate, thine eyes of mercy toward us. And, after this our exile, show unto us the blessed fruit of thy womb, Jesus. O clement, O loving, O sweet virgin Mary.

Pray for us, O holy mother of God

R. that we may be made worthy of the promises of Christ.

The Rosary Prayer

Let us pray.

R. O God, whose only-begotten Son by his life, death and resurrection, has purchased for us the rewards of eternal life; grant, we beseech thee, that by meditating upon these mysteries of the most holy Rosary of the Blessed Virgin Mary, we may imitate what they contain and obtain what they promise, through the same Christ our Lord. Amen.

Note: People will sometimes add other prayers as well, but these are the basic ones.

The Five Joyful Mysteries

The Annunciation
The Visitation
The Birth of Jesus
The Presentation
Finding the Child Jesus in the Temple

The Five Luminous Mysteries

The Baptism of Jesus in the River Jordan
The Wedding Feast at Cana
The Proclamation of the Kingdom of God
The Transfiguration of Jesus
The Institution of the Eucharist

The Five Sorrowful Mysteries

The Agony in the Garden
The Scourging at the Pillar
The Crowning with Thorns
The Carrying of the Cross
The Crucifixion of Jesus

The Five Glorious Mysteries

The Resurrection
The Ascension
Pentecost
The Assumption
The Crowning of Mary Queen of Heaven

The Joyful Mysteries are typically prayed on Monday and Saturday; the Luminous Mysteries on Thursday; the Sorrowful Mysteries on Tuesday and Friday; and the Glorious Mysteries on Wednesday and Sunday.

Your Rosary Beads

In my life, I have probably been gifted about a thousand rosaries. Most of them I have passed along to other people as gifts. There are all types of rosaries, from the simplest to the fanciest. I was once given a rosary made of solid gold as a thank-you gift for visiting the Cayman Islands. For about ten years I held on to it, until a bishop from a very poor diocese in Africa came to visit. Giving it to him, I explained what it was and said, "Keep it to pray with and to let your people pray with as a diocesan rosary, or sell it to pay for a priority need in your diocese. Either way I will know it has served your people, God's people, well."

There are, however, some rosaries that I have held on to, even though I never pray with them. First, there is the rosary that my teacher gave me in the fourth grade. It is a dark green knotted cord. In place of each bead is a knot, and it has a white plastic crucifix. It was made by an order of nuns in Papua New Guinea, a country in the South Pacific islands, just 125 miles off the northern tip of Australia. Then there are the rosaries given to me by Pope John Paul II and Pope Francis. But as I've said, the one I prefer to pray with is a simple wooden rosary. I have a lot of them: one in my bedside table, another in my car, one in my briefcase, one in my desk at the office, and another in my desk at home.

The beads make the Rosary a physical prayer as well as a spiritual prayer. The simple motion of moving your fingers from one bead to another creates a powerful rhythm. This physical motion and the rhythm it creates add to the soothing of your heart, mind, and soul that praying the Rosary produces. Great music is not just about the notes; just as important are the spaces between the notes. The beads are important because they represent the prayers, but the spaces between the beads are important too. Breathe during those spaces and allow the powerful rhythm to build. Otherwise there can be a tendency to rush. Once we start racing through the prayers, something is lost.

How to Use the Beads

A rosary has fifty-nine beads. Each bead corresponds with a prayer; some beads correspond with more than one prayer. The Rosary is made up of five decades. Each decade consists of one Our Father, ten Hail Marys, and one Glory Be. These account for fifty-five beads. There are also four introductory beads and a crucifix.

Following is a step-by-step explanation of what prayer (or prayers) to pray as you hold each bead. I have also included a diagram to provide further clarity.

This prayer has changed millions of lives. It has been a staple prayer for countless saints. May it change your life, help you to become the-very-best-version-of-yourself, and lead you to grow in virtue and live a holy life.

Bead *By* Bead:

Introductory Prayers

1. Crucifix. Make the Sign of the Cross and pray the Apostles' Creed.
2. Pray the Our Father; traditionally this is prayed for the intentions of the pope and the needs of the Church.
3. Pray the Hail Mary on each bead; traditionally these have been prayed for an increase in the three theological virtues: faith, hope, and charity.
4. Pray the Glory Be.

The Five Decades/Mysteries

5. Pray the Our Father on the medal. (For the remaining four decades, pray the Our Father on the bead between the decades.)
6. Pray the Hail Mary on each bead.
7. Pray the Glory Be on the space after the tenth bead.
8. Pray the Fatima Prayer (optional).
9. Repeat steps 5 through 8 for each of the four remaining decades/mysteries.

Closing Prayers

10. Pray the Hail Holy Queen.
11. Pray the Rosary Prayer.
12. Make the Sign of the Cross.

The *Joyful* Mysteries:

The Annunciation
Fruit of the Mystery: The Desire to Do God's Will

The Visitation
Fruit of the Mystery: Humble Service to Others

The Birth of Jesus
Fruit of the Mystery: Gratitude for Life

The Presentation
Fruit of the Mystery: Learning to Listen Deeply

Finding the Child Jesus in the Temple
Fruit of the Mystery: Wisdom

The First Joyful Mystery

The Annunciation

Fruit of the Mystery: The Desire to Do God's Will

Reflection:

Yes. It all comes down to that in the end. Are we willing to say yes to God? There are some beautiful lines in the Scriptures that sum everything up. On the wall in my children's room is a picture of Noah's ark, and inscribed in the wooden frame are the words "Noah did all that God asked him to do" (Genesis 7:5). That's it. Just do what God asks you to do. At the wedding feast in Cana, Mary said to the servants, "Do whatever he tells you" (John 2:5). Say yes to God in everything.

One moment at a time, we are each called to embrace his will. It is monumentally simple and monumentally difficult. But we find ways to complicate and avoid it.

Why don't we passionately seek God's will? All too often I find myself saying yes to God begrudgingly. It isn't a generous yes. I know that, and I know God knows it.

Mary puts me to shame. Her humble words of surrender, "Let it be it done unto me according to your word," echo throughout history as a spirituality unto themselves: Seek and do what you believe to be the will of God.

We should be a people of yes, generously saying yes to everything God calls us to. I cannot help but think, though, of those times when I have knowingly said no to God. They sting. And yet I know Mary would take me in her arms right now, hold me, encourage me, and send me out into the world inspired anew.

Let's begin again right now—a new beginning, a fresh commitment to say yes to God. And may these words never be far from our lips: "God, what do you think I should do in this situation?"

Prayer:

With these inspirations in our hearts and minds, we turn to you, Jesus, and pray.

Lord of every yes, give us wisdom to generously say yes to your way in the moments of the day; give us courage to turn our backs on anything that is not of you, no matter how enticing it may be to our senses or our ego.

You can take and you can give. Take from us the desire for anything that doesn't help us become the-best-version-of-ourselves, and give us the desire to do your will in all things. Give us the grace to say yes to you in the big things and the small things, in old ways and in new ways.

Jesus, we offer this decade to you for our family, living and deceased, wherever they are today, physically and spiritually. We ask you to fill them with the grace to take one step closer to you today. We also pray in a special way for every woman who found out she was pregnant today, and ask you to bless her with peace and hope.

Mary, pray for us and teach us to say yes to God in all things.

Amen.

The Second Joyful Mystery

The Visitation

Fruit of the Mystery: Humble Service to Others

Reflection:

When is the last time you responded to your spouse, parents, or customers "with all haste"? When your husband or wife asks you to do a chore, or when your manager at work asks you to do a little extra, do you respond with an enthusiasm to serve? We live in an age of meaninglessness, because we have lost sight of the fact that our very purpose is to serve God and others.

Mary rushed off to serve Elizabeth. It was her first reaction. Too often my first reaction is one of selfishness: "I don't feel like it"; "I'll do it later"; "Can't someone else take care of it?" But Mary had an instinct to serve, an ingrained humility.

God wants to fill us with a holy sense of urgency. Every day people are losing hope. God seems far from them. They feel forgotten, invisible, unloved. So much is at stake. Mary wants to teach us to love God and neighbor with this holy sense of urgency.

It's time to strive again to recognize God and his invitation to serve in life's ordinary moments. The Scriptures tell us that when Mary greets Elizabeth, the child John the Baptist leaps for joy in her womb. Even in the womb, John the Baptist recognizes he is in the presence of God. Too often, I get caught up in thoughts about my own needs or desires and become completely oblivious to God's presence in a situation or person.

There is a connection between this passage and an Old Testament passage in which David dances for joy before the ark of the covenant. For the Jewish people the ark of the covenant represents God's presence among them. Just as David danced for joy in the presence of God, we now see John the Baptist dancing for joy in the presence of God. At the moment, Mary was a human tabernacle ushering God into the presence of Elizabeth and John the Baptist—and their incredible awareness allowed them to recognize that astounding truth.

We have lost our senses. We have truly lost our spiritual senses. They have been dulled and drowned out by the chaos of our lives. Let's beg God to awaken and sharpen our spiritual senses so we can recognize him in every moment and dance for joy.

Prayer:
With these inspirations in our hearts and minds, we turn to you, Jesus, and pray.

Lord, fill us with a holy sense of urgency. Teach us to never put off an opportunity to share your love with others. Strip from us all complacency, laziness, and selfishness that prevent us from serving powerfully.

Inspire in us a love of service. Open our eyes and allow us to see serving others as a holy endeavor. Cast out our selfish desire to be served and replace it with a hunger to rediscover the meaning and purpose of our lives by putting others first.

Jesus, we offer this decade of the Rosary to you and your mother for our friends—past, present, and future. Reinvigorate us with the true spirit of friendship. We pray for the friends who love and encourage us today and the friends of other places and times in our lives with whom we have lost touch. We humbly ask that our prayer might give them the courage to take one step closer to you today. We also pray in a special way for all those who are lonely today and desperate for someone to visit them.

Mary, pray for us and teach us to recognize God at work in our lives.

Amen.

The Third Joyful Mystery

The Birth of Jesus

Fruit of the Mystery: Gratitude for Life

Reflection:

I love Christmas. People are different during this season. There seems to be more of a spirit of goodwill in the world. I am different. And I try to keep the spirit of Christmas alive throughout the year, but I fail again and again.

Let's exercise our spiritual senses and imagine that tonight is the night when Jesus is born. Place yourself there in Bethlehem on that holy night. The baby Jesus is lying there in the manger, with Mary and Joseph around him.

I will imagine myself as one of the shepherds. Who will you imagine yourself as? You are even keener to be with Jesus—you are one of the wise men. You have followed the star across the face of the earth just to have a few short moments with Jesus. There is a peace and a joy that are unattainable through the things of this world, and we find it here with Mary, Joseph, and the child Jesus. We spend time with the Holy Family. Time stands still. Have we been here for moments or for hours? How can being in their presence not change us?

As we leave, it strikes us. The world is a mess: war, poverty, corruption, greed, selfishness, violence, abuse, and injustice. The face of evil torments ordinary people every day. And God chose to put himself in the middle of our mess.

There are so many times when we try to avoid other people's messes. We judge: "It's your mess. You made it; you should clean it up." We justify: "People have to learn . . ." God's attitude is the complete opposite. He places himself right in the middle of our mess as the solution to it. We don't deserve it. We have no claim to it. God gives us a new beginning, a fresh start, freely and without merit.

Prayer:

With these inspirations in our hearts and minds, we turn to you, Jesus, and pray.

Lord, help us to be constantly aware that life is precious. Liberate us from our life-wasting habits so that we can live life to the fullest. Nudge us when we feel tempted to waste a day or an hour, or even a few minutes.

Remove any judgment from our hearts that causes us to think of ourselves as different from or better than others in any way. Warm our hearts so that we may see that it is within our power to help other people clean up their messes, and to act with the generous mercy you have shown us.

Jesus, we offer this decade to you for our own mothers—living or deceased—and for all mothers. We pray for all the children who will be born today. May they each have at least one person in their lives to teach them to walk with you. We pray in a special way for single mothers and for all those couples struggling to conceive a child, and for all parents who have lost a child.

Mary, pray for us and share your wisdom with all mothers.

Amen.

The Fourth Joyful Mystery

The Presentation

Fruit of the Mystery: Learning to Listen Deeply

Reflection:

Have you ever waited for something with great anticipation? Did you wait patiently? What are you waiting for in your life right now? Simeon had waited. This was his moment. He had waited patiently, and he had prayed patiently. Now he took baby Jesus in his arms.

Imagine the emotion as he pulled the child to his chest, his long gray beard caressing the child's head. His face filled with a strange combination of joy and anguish—joy for the present, anguish for the future he knew or sensed the child would face. The tears streaming down his face.

Put yourself there in the temple that day. Mary and Joseph have brought Jesus to present him to the Lord in obedience to the Jewish law. Mary, the Mother of God, submits her child to the Law of Moses. Think about it: They are presenting God to God, and yet they are obedient to the law. If anyone was ever exempt from a law, it was Jesus, Mary, and Joseph in this moment. But they chose obedience. This is a momentous act of humility.

How often do we decide that a particular rule or law doesn't apply to us? When we drive faster than the speed limit, neglect to declare some taxable income, or leave our phones on when we're on a plane or in a theater, we are really saying, "That law doesn't apply to me. That's for everyone else. I am above that law." This is our arrogance. "Poverty, chastity, and obedience. Obedience is by far the hardest to live," a wise old monk once told me. To whom are you willing to be obedient? We are allergic to the very word. It seems we are obedient only to our own desires. Addicted to comfort and convenience, we reject the very notion of obedience. No wonder we have such a hard time surrendering in obedience to the will of God.

The word *obedience* comes from the Latin word *obedire*, which means "to listen deeply." Mary listened deeply. Simeon listened deeply. By listening deeply they saw the wisdom of God's way.

Prayer:

With these inspirations in our hearts and minds, we turn to you, Jesus, and pray.

Lord, give us the patience of Simeon, knowing that often our impatience gets in the way of obedience; give us the grace necessary to see obedience as something that is life-giving rather than something that is oppressive. Help us to become a little more patient each day, and light a flame of desire for obedience in our hearts.

Inspire us to realize that your guidance, rules, and laws are designed in part to protect us from the great misery people experience when they reject your wisdom. And knowing that we cannot love you if we are not obedient to you, we present ourselves to you today just as Mary and Joseph presented Jesus. Instruct us in all things; guide us in all things; command us in all things; we desire to be your faithful servants.

Jesus, we offer this decade to you for the Church; help us together as the Church to meet people where they are and lead them to where you are calling them to be. We pray for all those involved in Catholic education, for religious orders, deacons, priests, bishops, and the pope.

We also pray in a special way for anyone who has been discouraged or hurt by the Church. We ask that you heal them by sending each and every one of them someone to love them out of their hurt.
Mary, pray for us and teach us to listen deeply to your son.

Amen.

The Fifth Joyful Mystery

Finding the Child Jesus in the Temple

Fruit of the Mystery: Wisdom

Reflection:

Have You Ever Lost Something?

When I think of Mary, I imagine someone very calm and peaceful, but now she is frantic. She is rushing from one place to another, asking people, "Have you seen Jesus?" The mild-mannered Joseph is shouting, "Jesus, Jesus!" The other people in the group become restless and disturbed; they have never seen Mary and Joseph like this either.

Think about when your wallet or your keys go missing. You panic at the possibility that they are lost or stolen, but most of the time you have just misplaced them. These are just things. Have you ever lost your child while shopping—even just lost sight of him or her for a few minutes? Your heart pounds; you feel like throwing up; you become frantic. God, the Creator of the Universe, entrusted Jesus the Messiah to Mary and Joseph's care—and they lost him. Imagine what they must have been thinking and how they were feeling: grief, torment, distress, anguish, torture.

And yet, so often we lose Jesus in our own lives and don't even notice. It might be days or weeks before we realize that we have lost him.

Word begins to spread of a boy teaching in the temple with astounding wisdom. The news reaches Mary and Joseph, and they rush to the temple. I follow them, trying to keep up, and as I enter the temple, I see you, sitting at Jesus' feet. Listening. Pondering. And with every word, he inspires you to be a better person and live a better life.

Prayer:

With these inspirations in our hearts and minds, we turn to you, Jesus, and pray.

Lord, help us to be constantly aware of your presence in our lives. Teach us to recognize you at work in the ordinary and extraordinary moments of life.

Just as it was perfectly natural for Jesus to be teaching in the synagogue, help me to find the one thing that you want me to passionately pursue. Free me of regret for lost time and fear of the future. Liberate me from the foolishness of thinking that I am too young or too old for you to work powerfully through me.

You made us for mission. You made us for service to others, and without this our lives seem empty and meaningless. Help us each to find our way to join you in ministry, whether that is greeting people warmly as they arrive at church on Sunday, starting a Bible study or a book club, or becoming a missionary in Africa, China, or right here in America.

Don't let us fall into the temptation of judging our mission and ministry. Help us to know that you have given us the perfect mix of talents and abilities to fulfill the mission you have designed for us.

Jesus, we offer this decade to you for everyone struggling to discover what exactly they should do with their lives. Give them insight and hope. And we pray in a special way for parents who have lost a child—for those whose child has died from illness or in war, been murdered or kidnapped. Ease their anguish. We pray also for those who have lost the right to see their children each day because of divorce or addiction.

Mary, pray for us and inspire in us the courage and perseverance to never stop seeking Jesus.

Amen.

The *Luminous* Mysteries:

The Baptism of Jesus in the River Jordan
Fruit of the Mystery: Healing of Body, Mind, and Soul

The Wedding Feast at Cana
Fruit of the Mystery: Generous Hospitality

The Proclamation of the Kingdom of God
Fruit of the Mystery: Desire for Holiness

The Transfiguration of Jesus
Fruit of the Mystery: Trust in God

The Institution of the Eucharist
Fruit of the Mystery: Belief in the True Presence of Jesus in the Eucharist

The First Luminous Mystery

The Baptism of Jesus in the River Jordan

Fruit of the Mystery: Healing of Body, Mind, and Soul

Reflection:

John the Baptist felt unworthy even to untie Jesus' sandals, but now Jesus stood in line with sinners and presented himself to John to be baptized. It seems to me that the more someone tries to grow spiritually, the more he or she struggles to embrace in a healthy way the unworthiness we all share. Teresa of Ávila counsels us: "Humility is truth." Jesus counsels us not to bury our talents or hide our light. Are we unworthy of God's love and infinite blessings? Yes. But that is only half the picture; the other half is that human beings are amazing and God loves us beyond comprehension.

When my first child was born, my spirituality was impacted significantly. I have always believed that God loves me. But when Walter was born, I began to experience the love of God in the very core of my soul.

I love my children more than I ever thought was possible before I had children. And here's the thing: I am weak and broken, fragile and flawed. But if I can love my children as much as I do, with all my limitations, imagine how much God loves his children—you and me! It all makes me feel unworthy. Yes, I feel blessed, and yet I often struggle with feelings of inadequacy and unworthiness. Some of this is natural and normal, healthy and good for us. But it is so easy to go too far and forget that as sons and daughters of the great King, and as his children, despite our unworthiness, we are invited by God to participate in all that his kingdom has to offer.

Prayer:
With these inspirations in our hearts and minds, we turn to you, Jesus, and pray.

Lord of truth and order, shine that truth and order upon us today so we can have and hold an honest and healthy sense of who we are and who we are not. Help us to see ourselves as you see us.
Let our self-esteem be based not upon the things we have done or not done, nor upon the things of this world that we have or don't have, nor upon our accomplishments or failures. Let our self-esteem be based upon the love you, your Father, and the Spirit shower upon us in every moment. Let it be the quiet, joyful confidence of a child who lives under the providence and protection of a powerful father.
Jesus, we offer this decade to you and your mother for every person, adult or child, who will be baptized today. Let the new life of baptism animate them for the rest of their lives. We also pray in a special way for people who lack the clarity or courage to live out the call of their baptism today. May there be better days ahead for them.

Mary, Mother of God and mother to us all, you are the most honored woman in history. Share with us your deep humility and steadfast confidence so that we can have a healthy sense of self.

Amen.

The Second Luminous Mystery

The Wedding Feast at Canna

Fruit of the Mystery: Generous Hospitality

Reflection:
Hospitality has been central to Christian culture from the very beginning. The first Christians perplexed and intrigued the people of their time with their radical hospitality, which was kind and generous, loving, thoughtful, and deeply personal in a tragically impersonal culture that treated most people like livestock. The hospitality of the first Christians made people feel welcome, and that is no small thing in a world filled with people hungry for acceptance and desperate to feel that they belong.

Weddings are a lavish expression of hospitality. Jesus and Mary were at a wedding. They did not seem to be very close to the newlyweds, and yet Mary and Jesus went to extraordinary lengths to prevent the new couple and their families from suffering the embarrassment of running out of wine.

Mary took hospitality so seriously that she asked her son to alter the events of history. Jesus obviously had a plan to begin his public life in some particular way at some particular time, and this was not it, but Mary asked him to change his plans. You recall that Jesus objected, saying it was not his time, and yet he ultimately complied with his mother's request. He denied himself, died unto himself, inconvenienced himself, and allowed his mother's request to change the course of salvation history. This alone shows us the incredible respect that Jesus had for Mary.

How do you react when people ask you to change your plans (in infinitely less significant ways)?

I've been reflecting on this mystery for thirty years, but something new just occurred to me. Mary must have known that Jesus could do something. Her request assumed that Jesus could solve the problem. How did she know? What extraordinary things had Mary seen Jesus do during the first thirty years of his life?

Every day we encounter opportunities to live our faith through hospitality. My wife and I like to make people feel so welcome when they stay with us that they never want to leave. As a leader of people at work, I see the workplace as a rich opportunity for hospitality with both our employees and customers; and I see Dynamic Catholic as a rich opportunity for radical hospitality with team members, donors, and customers. Each day presents a variety of invitations to extend kind and generous hospitality toward the people who cross our paths.

Next Sunday an out-of-town visitor will walk into your parish church for Mass. Will she feel welcomed? Will she walk away wishing that she and her family lived in the area so they could go to your church every Sunday because you made her feel so welcome?

Do you feel welcome in your own parish? Would a new parishioner feel welcome? How many people do you think don't really feel welcome in their parish?

Hospitality is a powerful ministry. Jesus never preached to anyone before he had addressed some human need. First he fed them, healed them, comforted them, made them feel like they belonged and were welcome. He opened their hearts to the divine by paying attention to their ordinary human needs.

Let's make our homes and parishes temples of welcome, temples of hospitality. People hear differently, respond differently, live differently, and give differently when they feel welcome.

Prayer:
With these inspirations in our hearts and minds, we turn to you, Jesus, and pray.

Lord, you inspired the first Christians to adopt generous hospitality as a way of life. By developing a rare awareness of other people's needs, they loved you by loving each other. In the process this generous hospitality helped them to build strong marriages and families, vibrant communities, and an identity in the broader culture that fascinated people.

Enrich all marriages and families with hospitality. Make us mindful of each other's needs and eager to serve them. Lord, use hospitality to renew marriage in our society. It is a practical and profound way to put the needs of others before our own. It demonstrates with action each day that we love each other. Inspire each marriage to become one of generous hospitality.

Jesus, we offer this decade to you for all married couples around the world; help them to appreciate each other. Give them courage to talk about the things that are difficult to talk about so their marriages can continue to grow.

We also pray in a special way for all couples getting married today; may the hope and joy of this day live on throughout their marriage. We pray for all engaged couples; give them the wisdom to prepare for marriage and not just plan a wedding. We pray also for those married couples celebrating their anniversary today, and we pray for any couple struggling in their marriage right now. We hold up to you all those who have suffered and continue to suffer the effects of divorce—the men, the women, and most especially the children. Finally, Jesus, we ask that just as you abundantly supplied more wine when it was in short supply at the wedding in Cana, please provide abundantly for whatever is in short supply in our lives today.

Mary, in Cana you displayed the awareness of hospitality. Help us to become more aware every single day of what is happening within us and around us. Especially increase our awareness of the needs of others.

Amen.

The Third Luminous Mystery

The Proclamation of the Kingdom of God

Fruit of the Mystery: Desire for Holiness

Reflection:

When Jesus spoke about the kingdom, he perplexed people. They had a certain image of God and his ways, and Jesus turned it upside down and inside out. In our own ways, we too have images of God and ways of thinking about how he does things that he wants to turn upside down—which, as it turns out, will be right side up.

The kingdom is different. God's ways are not man's ways. The first will be last. All men, women, and children are equal—the rich and the poor, the healthy and the sick, the young and the old. The world lusts for power and might, while the kingdom of God is ruled by truth, beauty, and goodness. The currency of a worldly kingdom is money and influence, but the currency of God's kingdom is kindness, compassion, and mercy. The world seeks control; God loves freedom. The world is motivated by self-interest, while the kingdom of God invites us to set aside our own interests to pursue the will of God and lay down our life for others. The world worships possessions and accomplishments; the kingdom says who you become is infinitely more important than what you do or what you have. The world seeks ever more; the kingdom says less is more. The world complicates; the kingdom simplifies. The world lusts, while the kingdom loves. The world confuses, but the kingdom clarifies. The world hates enemies; the kingdom has no enemies because we love our enemies until they become one with us. The world is divided; the kingdom is united.

The kingdom of God looks and acts like Jesus. It is a kingdom of outrageous generosity.

Everyone needs the kingdom. It's a place; it's a person; it's a worldview; it's the question and the answer; it's the ultimate system of values. And it is to be sought unrelentingly.

Jesus came to reveal the kingdom of God to us so we could live loving and just lives in the eyes of God. He stays at our side, encouraging and challenging us, so that we can live up to the promise of baptism, live more loving and just lives, and in the process make our tiny corner of the world more loving and just.

Jesus invites us to live in this world in a kingdom way. Is your life making the world more like the kingdom of God? How are you proclaiming the kingdom of God in your own life?

Prayer:
With these inspirations in our hearts and minds, we turn to you, Jesus, and pray.

Lord of this world and the next, help us to see this world for what it is and open our spiritual senses to see the next world as it is: something worth living and dying for.

Give us the courage to join you in the mission to bring about the reign of your kingdom here on earth as it is in heaven. Inspire each of us in our way to see our vocation as a way to bring your love and justice to each and every situation in our lives. Give us courage when courage is needed. Give us clear thinking and compelling words when clear thinking and compelling words are needed. Give us silence when silence is needed. Give us humility when others seek to humiliate us and the kingdom. Remind us daily that it is impossible to help you build your kingdom when we are so obsessed with building our own.

Rearrange our priorities around your kingdom's priorities. Give us kingdom values, and inspire us to live them. Teach us a kingdom way of doing things, and let our goals be kingdom goals.

Jesus, we offer this decade to you for anyone actively seeking his or her mission in life. Let these people hear your voice in their lives more clearly today than ever before. We pray for those who are confused about how they should live their lives. Give them the grace of light and the wisdom of patience and free them from the devil of inaction.

We also pray in a special way for the mentally ill. We beg you to soothe their minds, bodies, and souls so they may find relief from their troubles. Give those who care for them comfort and patience. Their roles are difficult, emotionally draining, require long hours, and are often thankless; send others into their lives to thank and appreciate them.

Mary, teach us to love the kingdom and embrace kingdom values; increase our desire for the kingdom to reign in every situation, in our thoughts and actions, in our hearts, minds, souls, and lives.

Amen.

The Fourth Luminous Mystery

The Transfiguration

Fruit of the Mystery: Trust in God

Reflection:

Why Moses and Elijah? Elijah represents all the prophets who yearned for the coming of Jesus. Moses is the giver of the Law. Why not Abraham, who received the promise of the Messiah and is our father in faith? One explanation is that Jesus came to fulfill the prophets and the law. The law outlined the problem of sin, and Jesus was the solution to that problem . . . and so much more.

What is the problem in your life? Are you allowing Jesus to be the solution? Are you looking at the problem from a divine perspective? Or are you looking at it from an earthly perspective and trying to solve it with your own might?

Jesus wants to show us what is possible. Too often our vision is too earthbound. He wants to open our hearts and minds to all that is possible, far beyond our limited thinking.

God is constantly trying to help us see things as they really are. The disciples, like you and I, could see Jesus only in a very limited way because of their limits. Jesus took Peter, John, and James up on the mountain so God the Father could open their spiritual eyes wider than ever before and help them see Jesus in all his glory.

God is also constantly trying to help us to see possibilities that we don't see because of our blind spots, low self-esteem, attachment to a particular path or outcome, and other flaws and limitations. Most of the time we don't see many of the options and possibilities that exist for us in a situation.

Most people have many more options than they see when making choices. We settle so easily on one or two options and then think the great dilemma is to decide between the two. But the reality is that there may be a dozen more that we are not yet aware of, because we lack the patience necessary to take inventory of all the options available to us in that situation. Sometimes we will agonize about it and sincerely struggle to choose between the two, when in truth what God is really inviting us to didn't even make our list of options because we were in too much of a rush. You always have more options than you think you do.

How would your priorities change if you saw yourself as you really are? How would you live differently?

God wants you to see things differently. He wants you to see all that you are capable of doing, being, and becoming. With this new sense of yourself, he wants you to live differently.

Prayer:
With these inspirations in our hearts and minds, we turn to you, Jesus, and pray.

Lord of possibilities, open our physical and spiritual eyes to see all the opportunities before us in every situation. Lord, help us to really see. Nudge us when we are tempted to limit ourselves and settle for less than who you made us to be. Remove the blind spots of ego, fear, ambition, prejudice, and bias, and help us to see things as they really are—and as they truly can be. Transform us into people of possibility.

Now that we are ablaze with a sense of all that is possible, help us to realize what Leon Bloy observed: "The only real sadness, the only real failure, the only great tragedy in life, is not to become a saint." In every moment of every day, remind us, Lord, that holiness is possible. And give us the courage to collaborate with you to transform each moment of life into a holy moment.

Jesus, we offer this decade of the Rosary for everyone enduring much greater problems and challenges than our own. Give them comfort, and give us compassion.

We also pray in a special way for the quiet and anonymous saints in the world who go about their days bringing joy, hope, and comfort to everyone who crosses their path. At times they too must experience discouragement and disappointment. At those times, send someone to encourage them and fill them with your energy and enthusiasm for life once more. Thank you for their example of holiness in the world. They remind us that holiness is indeed possible for ordinary people. Mary, help us to see your son as he really is, was, and ever will be.

Amen.

The Fifth Luminous Mystery

The Institution of the Eucharist

Fruit of the Mystery: Belief in the True Presence of Jesus in the Eucharist

Reflection:

What We Don't Know

Indifference toward the Eucharist is one of the marks of our age. It is so easy to become indifferent—toward people, toward things of great value, and even indifferent toward life itself. It's human nature. If we do not intentionally and proactively foster the awe and respect that God, the Church, the Mass, the Eucharist, and life deserve, our hearts will become indifferent to these treasures.

Observe the attitude and behavior of Catholics at Mass, and the only conclusion you can reach is that they are indifferent toward Jesus, the Son of the living God, the King of Kings and Lord of Lords, the beginning and the end, the God-man who died for them on the cross and saved them from their sins—the same Jesus who shows us all how to be reasonably happy in this life and invites us to join him in the supreme happiness of eternity.

We live in an age of indifference. We shouldn't be surprised. If people en masse can be indifferent toward Jesus, nobody is safe from their prideful indifference.

Have you ever helped somebody, really gone above and beyond to make his life better, but then afterward he resented you? His indifference toward you stings at first, but as you reflect on all you did for him, the pain goes way beyond a shallow sting; it goes deep to the core of your heart and soul. You are shocked and appalled, but you shouldn't be. We all do it. Worst of all, we do it to God.

In a culture of indifference, nothing is holy. This is what we see in the way people speak to and treat each other, in the way anyone or anything that is good and holy is attacked.

The Mass and the Eucharist should inspire awe and a deep respect. I admit that they often don't for me. That is proof of my ignorance. The Mass and the Eucharist are ever-fresh, ever-new fountains of wisdom, love, mercy, and grace. We could go to Mass every day of our lives, and there would still be an infinite number of lessons we could learn from the Mass and the Eucharist.

One reason for our indifference is that this cynical world has dulled our spiritual senses. Our spiritual imagination and spiritual sight have both been accosted by the subtle and not-so-subtle daily attacks of our culture.

Do you know what happened at the Last Supper? If we consider this question, most of us would say yes and then recite the facts and mechanics of that historic experience. In our arrogant foolishness we think we know what happened at the Last Supper.

Let's consider what we don't know about the Last Supper. Who arrived first? Who was the last to leave? Which disciple was most concerned that the others had what they needed? What were Andrew and Peter talking about that night? What was Judas thinking as he prepared to betray his brothers and his God? Were the disciples talking about the future, making plans that would never materialize because in a matter of hours the world would change forever? Were they arguing about something trivial or inconsequential? How did that make Jesus feel, knowing what he knew about what was about to happen? Which of the disciples had the best sense of humor? Were they joking around that night before dinner, oblivious to the fact that they were about to experience one of the most serious events in the history of the world? Did they know that future generations would be able to consume the body and blood of Jesus? Did they know that people would kill and be killed over this single idea, that it would be the solitary truth that would cause so many to abandon Jesus?

Do you know what happened at the Last Supper? What we don't know about it dwarfs what we do know. What we don't know about God makes what we do know about him look like a grain of sand in the Sahara.

Let us beg Jesus to awaken our spiritual senses so that as we read the Scriptures we can smell the dust rising from the road, hear the whispers in the crowd as he speaks, notice the looks on various people's faces, and hear his words without the noise and distractions of this world.

It's amazing what we choose to focus on in our lives. It's astounding what we choose to care about. Put whatever you are worried about right now in the big picture of God, life, the history of the world, and eternity. The things we choose to make important often reveal our distorted priorities.

Indifference is a destroyer of love. Indifference often prevents love from beginning, for it places us inside an impregnable shell of uncaring.

Prayer:
With these inspirations in our hearts and minds, we turn to you, Jesus, and pray.

Lord, draw us nearer to you than ever before. Inspire us to spend time with you before the tabernacle. When the opportunity is available to spend time with you in adoration, let us embrace it. We also ask you to arrange things so that we can attend Mass more often and receive you—body, blood, soul, and divinity—in the humble host.

Banish indifference from our hearts and our lives.

Fill us today with a whole new love and respect for the power of the Eucharist. Lord, take our minuscule understanding of what the Eucharist is and what it can do to a whole new level. Somehow, somewhere, sometime, let this great divider unite all Christians and the whole world in peace and tranquility.

Jesus, we offer this decade to you for priests: for every priest who is, for every priest who has been, and for every priest who will be. Bless them, Lord, with grace unimaginable to carry out their work. Never let them doubt the importance of their work and the difference it makes for ordinary people who seek to love you, do your will, and live good lives. Lift them up when they are discouraged. Raise up in them a deep desire to heal your people, and teach them to take care of their bodies and souls just as you did.

We also pray in a special way for all those who are preparing to be priests and to minister to your people, for all those who are discerning a call to the priesthood—please give them courage. And for any priest, or any person, who has lost faith in your true presence in the Eucharist, give each of them new energy for life and ministry and new courage to share your love and your message with others.

Lord, help us to realize what we are really hungry for in our lives today, and give us the wisdom to realize that you want to feed our deepest needs with the Eucharist.

Mary, just as the priest prays, "O Priest of God, pray this Mass as if it were your first Mass, your last Mass, your only Mass," help us to approach each Mass with great respect and wonder, as if it were our first Mass, our last Mass, our only Mass.

Amen.

The *Sorrowful* Mysteries:

The Agony in the Garden
Fruit of the Mystery: Sorrow for Sin

The Scourging at the Pillar
Fruit of the Mystery: Compassion

The Crowning with Thorns
Fruit of the Mystery: Patience

The Carrying of the Cross
Fruit of the Mystery: Courage to Face Injustice

The Crucifixion of Jesus
Fruit of the Mystery: Redemption

The First Sorrowful Mystery

The Agony in the Garden

Fruit of the Mystery: Sorrow for Sin

Reflection:

You and I are there, in the garden with Jesus. The sky is dark but clear, and the air is crisp. Imagine for this meditation that you and I are two of Jesus' disciples, just a stone's throw away from him, but we grow weary and fall asleep. When Jesus comes back and wakes us, we are ashamed of ourselves. We feel weak and regretful. Jesus doesn't make us feel this way; we make ourselves feel these things.

Stay awake. He says it three times. But we cannot. We let him down. Imagine how alone he feels this night in the garden. We have added to his intense aloneness by not being able to even keep watch during these last hours with him.

Has anything changed today?

I still fall asleep today. Sometimes I fall asleep when I am praying. Perhaps Jesus is speaking to me through that experience and telling me I need more rest. But I sense he is more likely saying to me, "Why did you put your prayer off all day until the afternoon or evening?" or "Shouldn't you give prayer your best time and your best energy?" He has mentioned these things to me so many times before, and naturally I am disappointed in myself that he has to tell me once more. So I make a resolution to give prayer more priority in my life.

I fall asleep in other ways too. Some days I fall asleep in my marriage, or as a parent. There are times when I have been asleep for weeks or months with regard to physical fitness. It's so easy to take a nap from financial responsibility. God instructs us, as pilgrims who are just passing through this place we call earth, to stay awake and be constantly vigilant and attentive to what matters most, rather than letting what matters least take over our schedules and lives.

It is so easy to judge the disciples for falling asleep after Jesus specifically asked them to stay awake to pray and watch with him. In the Gospels Jesus went off to pray alone often. Perhaps the disciples thought it was just another one of those times, not realizing that this time was different, not knowing that this would be the last time.

And don't we all fall asleep in different ways in our lives when God is calling us to stay awake and be mindful of everything that is going on around us and within us?

Have you ever been in agony—physical, spiritual, emotional, psychological? Multiply that by infinity and take it to the depths of eternity, and you may get a small glimpse of what Jesus was experiencing that night in the Garden of Gethsemane.

When was the last time you spent an hour in prayer? It might be time again.

Prayer:

With these inspirations in our hearts and minds, we turn to you, Jesus, and pray.

Lord, in the garden that night you prayed openly and honestly to the Father with so much intensity that you began to sweat blood. I suppose it all comes down to the fact that you knew what was at stake. Too often I forget what is at stake.

It is impossible to ignore that I put you there in that garden that night. This realization ignites a set of emotions that begin with shame and embarrassment and end with sheer horror. You are paying for the careless debts I have amassed. My stomach turns when I consider that this is just the beginning of your total surrender to redeem me, my friends and family, colleagues at work, childhood schoolmates . . . and all of humanity.

I want to look away, run away, but I can't. You are sweating blood, and I know this is only the beginning. Nobody has even laid a hand on you yet. The anguish of all that has been and will be causes even you to wonder if there could be another way.

Worst of all, I struggle some days to even be sorry for some of my sins. There are still areas of my life that I don't surrender to you or even allow you to enter. Why don't I trust you more? Why don't I believe that everything is better done your way?

The ugly truth is that I love some of my sins. I don't want to give those particular sins up. I plan my days around them. Lord of everything that is good, true, and beautiful, help me to see that your way is the best way in all things—and help me then to give up the sins I love. This scares me. I am certain there will be slips and falls, disappointments and failures. So first, give me desire. Give me the desire to be sorry for my sins and the desire to give up the sins I refuse to give up. Let that desire grow stronger and stronger every time I do anything kind, generous, thoughtful, or compassionate for anyone. In this way I can collaborate with you to get that flame of desire to burn like a raging fire in my heart and soul.

Jesus, we offer this decade to you for everyone around the world praying the Rosary today. Allow us to see with clarity what you are calling us to next, and give us the courage to carry it out day by day.

Mary, Mother of the same Jesus who was arrested in the garden; the same Jesus who did not resist their unjust arrest; the same Jesus who will suffer and die to renew our relationship with God; whisper in our ear each time we are tempted to sin. Whisper words of wisdom and encouragement, whisper to us the reality of the next world, so we can turn our backs on sin and strive evermore to live a life of virtue.

Amen.

The Second Sorrowful Mystery

The Scourging at the Pillar

Fruit of the Mystery: Compassion

Reflection:

One sentence. "Then Pilate took Jesus and had him flogged." Eight words. But this would have been enough to kill most people. The flesh on his back was torn in a hundred places, blood dripping from each small piece of his divine body ripped off and scattered on the floor—the body of Christ. Still, this was almost nothing compared to what he was to go through.

Why are we so cruel to each other? There is a cruel streak that runs through humanity. You can see it in small children playing together on the playground. They will ignore or exclude another child, push another child around and laugh about it, or insult a child by calling him names or by making fun of what he is wearing.

Adults are often no better. Our insecurities result in cruelty toward others in many ways: gossip, exclusion, arguing unnecessarily, negative humor, defamation, bullying. These are just some of the everyday ways we human beings are cruel to each other. A cursory examination of history or the crimes committed in any city each week shows that our capacity to be cruel to each other has no bounds. This cruelty demands that we objectify the person we are being cruel to in some way, to think of him or her as less than fully human.

And yet, while we each have an overwhelming desire to be treated as a unique human being, we often ignore other people's humanity and treat them according to the function they play in our lives. Do you treat the person who serves you at a restaurant as a person or as a server? Ever wonder what is going on in that person's life? His grades might be suffering because he has to work so many hours just to pay for school and doesn't have enough time to study. She might have just had a miscarriage. He might have just found out that his dad has cancer. But most of all, like we all do from time to time, she might just be having a bad day for no particular reason. Functionalizing people—treating them according to their function instead of treating them as human beings—is a subtle and cunning form of cruelty.

Jesus didn't functionalize people. That's why we find so many people from the fringes of society at the center of so many Gospel stories. He didn't treat the prostitute like a prostitute; he treated her like a unique human being made in the image of God. He didn't reduce the tax collector to his function and treat him like a tax collector. He didn't treat the Samaritan like a Samaritan. He didn't treat the adulterer like an adulterer. He didn't treat the thief like a thief.

Jesus didn't think of the man who was scourging him as a cruel and angry beast. He thought of him as a human being, uniquely and wonderfully made. He saw the whole picture. He saw him perhaps as a desperate man trapped in a brutal system, trying to support his wife and children, struggling to survive in a culture that was harsh, impersonal, and cruel—especially to those with no power, money, rank, or position.

Now consider this: Who is the one person you have loved more than any other in your life? Jesus loved the man who scourged him more than that. Jesus loved that man more than you and I have ever loved anyone.

Prayer:

With these inspirations in our hearts and minds, we turn to you, Jesus, and pray.

Lord, teach me to love like you. There are so many obstacles that get in the way of loving like you: my selfishness and insecurities; my pride and unwillingness to forgive; my anger and envy; my lust and gluttony; my greed and laziness. Fill me with the grace to pray and fast more than ever before in my life, and cast these obstacles aside so that each day I can love more and more like you.

Help me to never judge, objectify, or functionalize people, but to see each and every person whose path I cross as you see them.

Jesus, we offer this decade to you for the man who scourged you at the pillar long ago and far away. We pray for anyone who feels trapped in a way of life that is self-destructive, sinful, and hurtful to others. Lord of liberty, open a door, break a window, dig a tunnel, crash through a wall, construct a bridge, part the sea, build a road . . . and lead each and every one of these trapped souls to a new and better life. Give them hope and fulfill that hope. We will help; just show us how.

We also pray in a special way for anyone who has been unjustly accused and punished for something they didn't do. Raise them above these painful circumstances and somehow keep their hearts from hardening with anger and resentment. Hold them in your arms and comfort them in ways beyond human imagination. Stir the conscience of anyone who can set matters right so that justice can be celebrated no matter how long it has been.

Mary, model of patience, our impatience prevents us from loving people as we could and should. Teach us uncommon and extraordinary patience so that we can love every person in every situation as you and your son did and do.

Amen.

The Third Sorrowful Mystery

The Crowning with Thorns

Fruit of the Mystery: Patience

Reflection:

It seems we will do anything to avoid pain and suffering today. But not Jesus. He embraced every experience of pain and suffering. Why the great difference between God's approach and the world's approach?

The world believes that suffering is meaningless and should be avoided at all costs. God believes that suffering has value. If suffering has no value, then it is such a waste of life, but if it does have value, the waste is even greater if we don't channel it toward some higher purpose.

They crowned him with thorns and used a stick to smack the crown down on his head, driving the thorns deep into his scalp. He felt it all. He accepted it all. He embraced it all. He allowed each thorn, each taunt to strengthen his resolve to do what was before him on that day when the world went dark and cold.

We don't need to go looking for suffering. There is enough inevitable and unavoidable suffering in our lives. But let's start learning from this suffering, allowing it to be a source of spiritual growth.

There is a whole continuum of suffering. At one end you have something as common as inconvenience. At the other end you have something as horrible as the death of a child. By going deep into the smaller forms rather than running from them, by embracing the lesser forms of unavoidable suffering, we allow this hideous aspect of life to strengthen our will so we can choose what is good, true, and right in the moments of our lives—but this spiritual practice of embracing suffering prepares us for greater suffering that may be in our future.

Long before Jesus was arrested in the Garden of Gethsemane, he had been preparing for all that his arrest set in motion. For thirty years before the wedding in Cana, he had been preparing for the end. Throughout his public life, he suffered in ways we will never know, and it all prepared him for fifteen hours that began with his arrest and ended with his death. Jesus being arrested and humiliated, scourged at the pillar, and crowned with thorns were small compared to what was ahead—and yet, these things prepared him and strengthened him spiritually to fully carry out his mission.

This is the Savior of the world. Look how we treated him. We ignored him, humiliated him, mocked him, scourged his flesh, spat on him, drove thorns into the tender skin around his head—but we were not finished yet.

The crown of thorns driven into his head—I did that. This is not pious talk; I know it to be true. My personal actions led to his personal suffering.

And we do it again today. With our thoughts, words, actions, or inaction, we do it again today—and not only to Jesus, but to others. Why? This is the great unspoken truth: because we love this world, we love some of our sins, and we are addicted to comfort. We love these things more than God, more than ourselves, and more than the people we love the most.

Have you ever known somebody who really changed his or her life? It doesn't happen very often. People will change in small ways, or even overhaul one aspect of their lives. But Jesus is inviting us to a radical transformation. Most people don't believe it is possible or that they are capable. Show them. Why don't you be the one to show them it is possible?

Prayer:

With these inspirations in our hearts and minds, we turn to you, Jesus, and pray.

Lord, you suffered so that we might have life and have it to the fullest. Fill us with a deep gratitude for all you have done for us, and inspire us to show our gratitude by actually living life to the fullest.

Just as you suffered so we could have a more abundant life, fill us with a desire to make sacrifices so others can live more fully. Liberate us from our attachment to comfort so we can help others live in the dignity of work, with a home that is clean and safe, and food to nourish mind, body, and soul. If giving up some of our comfort is enough to bring real dignity to others who are on the fringes of society, why are we waiting?

Lord, help us to stop confusing our wants with needs. Help us to realize that there is an order to all you do. Help us to see clearly that needs are primary and wants are secondary—whether those needs are our own or somebody else's.

Jesus, we offer this decade to you for anyone who suffers unnecessarily—physically, mentally, or spiritualty. Give us the courage to step beyond our comfort zones to do as much as we can with what we have, where we are—and to encourage others to do the same.

Mary, help us to set aside comfort and convenience occasionally and put the needs of others ahead of our wants.

Amen.

The Fourth Sorrowful Mystery

The Carrying of the Cross

Fruit of the Mystery: Courage to Face Injustice

Reflection:

The Scriptures invite us deeper and deeper into every story each time we read or ponder them. Let's consider Judas for a moment. Is he just the villain of the Gospel? Have you ever learned anything from him? Have you ever considered it from his point of view? Are you like Judas in any way?

The betrayal of Jesus by Judas is a tragedy, but not just in the obvious way. It is also a tragedy that Jesus lost one of his disciples. Imagine how much that broke Jesus' heart. Judas had been chosen to be one of the twelve who would go out and change the world.

I wonder what Judas was like in the days leading up to the betrayal.

Did he start to distance himself from the other disciples? Was he visiting with old friends in Jerusalem? Did he begin to isolate himself from everyone and everything? Did he do or say anything that gave the disciples clues about what he was thinking?

They were so used to all being together. Maybe James and John thought he was with Peter and Matthew, and perhaps Peter and Matthew thought he was with some of the other disciples. So Judas may have felt all alone and may have been all alone. But why did he do it? Was Jesus just too different from his vision of the Messiah? Was he not getting enough attention? Did he feel he should have a greater leadership among the disciples? Was he exhausted from the life of ministry, seduced by the things of this world? How did Judas deceive himself?

Every sin leaves behind so many unanswered questions. Whatever the reason, Judas betrayed Jesus, broke his heart—and then killed himself and broke Jesus' heart again.

Now we are following Jesus as he carries his cross. We look at his face and deep into his eyes and wonder how he is even still alive, and he collapses. Simon of Cyrene is accosted by the guards and then helps Jesus carry his cross as if he himself were a criminal.

The Rosary is ever new because the situations and mysteries we are pondering have an unlimited number of dimensions to consider.

I wonder who made Jesus' cross. He was just doing his job, making a living to support his wife and children. Did he know it was for Jesus? How did he feel about making it? Did he feel guilty or was he completely oblivious? Or perhaps as the days and weeks went by, his role in the crucifixion led him to think about Jesus and who he really was and eventually he became a Christian. We don't know.

The point is, somebody made Jesus' cross. But it wasn't just the woodworker with his tools and hands; we made it with our sins.

Prayer:

With these inspirations in our hearts and minds, we turn to you, Jesus, and pray.

Lord, help me to carry my cross with grace and dignity, knowing that you are shouldering the burden with me.

Liberate me from selfishly seeking comfort constantly. Open my eyes spiritually so that I can see how the cross in all its forms helps me become the-best-version-of-myself.

Jesus, we offer this decade to you for anyone suffering from any form of injustice. We humans have invented so many ways to be unkind, unjust, and cruel. Help us to seek justice for ourselves and others, even when it comes at great personal cost. We also pray in a special way for the mentally ill. Many of us will never understand the cross they carry; please give us the grace to be kind and gentle with them.

Mary, what were you thinking and feeling that day? Did those images stab your heart every day for the rest of your life? Did you wake in the night sweating from the terror of reliving those moments in nightmares? Pray for us, Mary. Teach us to prayerfully endure unavoidable suffering and to comfort others when they suffer.

Amen.

The Fifth Sorrowful Mystery

The Crucifixion of Jesus

Fruit of the Mystery: Redemption

Reflection:

When people stop thinking for themselves and groupthink takes control, the outcome is usually inhumane. Never was that more true than in the case of Jesus' condemnation, torture, execution, and death.

Consider the pain of a nail being driven through your wrist—just one small part of our Lord's passion. Suffering reminds us, perhaps more than anything else, that God's ways are not ours. We live in a secular culture that despises suffering as useless and proclaims that it should be avoided at all costs. As a result, pain relievers are constantly being thrust at us in the form of pills, products, experiences, and distractions.

The world has its own gospel. The message of the world is incomplete, and nothing demonstrates this incompleteness more than the world's inability to make sense of suffering. The world cannot make sense of suffering because it views suffering as worthless. The world has no answer for the inescapable, unavoidable, and inevitable suffering of our lives.

Central to this dilemma the gospel of the world faces is its inability to make sense of death. It encourages us to live in denial of death, which may be the height of the lunacy of this false gospel.

Jesus has an answer for everything. In the Old Testament Scriptures suffering is often presented as the consequence of people's sinfulness; suffering was the result of ignoring God's teachings. In some cases punishment was presented as being inflicted by God as a direct result of humanity's sinfulness. In the New Testament, Jesus boldly announces with his words and actions that suffering has value. It is a tool that can transform us into more loving people. It ushers us into higher spiritual realms. Salvation and the suffering of Jesus are inseparable. So what could be more meaningful than suffering?

What was Jesus hoping to achieve by dying on the cross? What were the dreams that gave him courage and the perseverance to go through with it? I suspect his hopes and dreams were many and beautiful. Let's consider one. He hoped his life and death would change what people placed at the center of their lives. What's at the center of your life? Money, sex, food, drugs, shopping, image, ego, and control—or the outrageous generosity, service, and love of God and neighbor that Jesus proposed?

Someone told me once that being in debt, the kind of debt you know you will never be able to pay, gives you this constant feeling like you can't breathe. There is a time and place for everything in God's plan, and every debt in the universe needs to be settled eventually. This day two thousand years ago was the time and Calvary was the place that God decided to settle our debts.

And, of course, Jesus' answer to death is resurrection, redemption, and eternal life.

Prayer:

With these inspirations in our hearts and minds, we turn to you, Jesus, and pray.

Lord, you give and take according to our needs and your wisdom. On this dark day you laid down your life to give us all a fresh start, a new beginning, and a never-ending stream of marvelous grace and beautiful mercy.

Give us the wisdom, Jesus, to use the minds you gave us to think for ourselves; teach us to develop and listen to our conscience, avoid groupthink; fill us with courage to avoid mob behavior and instead stand up for justice.

When we suffer ourselves, help us to offer that suffering to you for worthy intentions. Never let us waste our suffering by getting caught up in self-pity.

Jesus, we offer this decade to you for anyone who is suffering physically today. We ask you to fill them with the rare grace necessary to see and experience suffering as a way to get closer to you. We pray for all those we have wronged in our lives, and for those who have wronged us. We also pray in a special way for everyone who will die today. Hold them in their transition from this life to the next, and comfort their loved ones as you comforted and consoled so many people while you walked the earth.

Mary, pray for us and teach us to trust your son.

Amen.

The *Glorious* Mysteries:

The Resurrection
Fruit of the Mystery: Faith

The Ascension
Fruit of the Mystery: Desire for Heaven

Pentecost
Fruit of the Mystery: Friendship with the Holy Spirit

The Assumption
Fruit of the Mystery: Aging and Dying Gracefully

The Crowning of Mary Queen of Heaven
Fruit of the Mystery: True Devotion to Mary

The First Glorious Mystery

The Resurrection

Fruit of the Mystery: Faith

Reflection:

Looking in All the Wrong Places

God does his greatest work in the midst of our greatest darkness. It is when our hearts are broken that God does some of his best work. How did the disciples feel that Friday night? Defeated and hopeless. Lost and confused. Swallowed by an all-encompassing darkness. How did they feel on Saturday? Brokenhearted perhaps. They say the darkest hour is right before the dawn, and it is in these darkest hours that God is often preparing to do his greatest work. He certainly was that Sunday morning.

Looking back on life I can see that time and time again, I was looking in the wrong places for all sorts of things. Here we find the women who loved and cared for Jesus throughout his public life looking for him in the wrong places.

The interesting thing is that Jesus had made himself clear. He had spoken using a metaphor when he said, "Destroy this temple, and in three days I will raise it up." He was telling his followers and everyone that would listen that on the third day he would rise from the dead. It was the third day—why were they so surprised? Did they not believe him? And even if they didn't understand Jesus when he first said it, here, now, in the face of the reality of the Resurrection, did they still not get it?

Whatever the case may be, it seems that since the very beginning humanity has been looking for love and happiness in all the wrong places. Are we looking for the abundant life in the wrong places today?

Now let's put ourselves there, in Jerusalem on that Sunday morning. Imagine how quickly word spread. Imagine how many versions of the story were circulating. The city would have been filled with emotion like never before: joy, anger, fear, confusion, anxiety, frustration, rage, indifference, hatred, and others. What were the Pharisees feeling when they first heard? How did it make Pilate feel? Were the men who tortured and executed him afraid he would come back for revenge? And no doubt there were many who went on with their lives indifferently, thinking he was just another man and accepting the story that his followers had stolen his body.

It must have been some Sunday morning. The city would have been drowning in gossip and emotion. But few if any would have recognized that this was the main event of human history. Jesus rose from the dead.

On that day there were no doubt many who ignored it, and many others who doubted it, rejected it, or were skeptical or cynical. These people have existed in every age and exist today, but you see them wandering through their lives confused. It is simply impossible to make sense of life and history without acknowledging the Resurrection.

You and I are walking through the streets of Jerusalem, listening to people talk about it on that Sunday morning. Do we believe? Do we have doubts? Are we too busy attending to the urgent matters of our lives to even care?

We keep walking and decide to visit the tomb. The place is crowded, and there are guards trying to keep people away. But we stand there for a few moments quietly and wonder, What does all this mean?

Now returning to the present, what part of your life needs resurrecting today? Do you want Jesus to resurrect that part of your life? Or are you attached to the dysfunction and self-destruction?

It's time to live in the risen Lord. When we do, we are fully alive; we experience joy and ecstasy, detachment from the passing troubles of this world, and confidence that in the end truth and goodness will always prevail.

On Friday afternoon they nailed Truth and Goodness to a tree. But on Sunday morning Truth rose from the dead. You cannot kill Truth and Goodness. You can put it in a tomb, but you cannot keep it there.

Prayer:

With these inspirations in our hearts and minds, we turn to you, Jesus, and pray.

Lord, unleash the power of the Resurrection in my life today. Resurrect the area of my life that most needs it today. Help me to stop resisting your grace, stay out of your way, and let you work in me and through me in whatever ways you want.

Your Resurrection demands a response, Jesus. You have conquered death and hatred with love. Teach us to do the same in some small way in our own lives. Give us the courage to love when we are rejected, despised, hated, ignored, bullied, abused, unappreciated, and taken for granted.

Thank you, Jesus. Thank you. I pray I never let a day pass without these words crossing my lips.

Jesus, we offer this decade to you for all those who have lost faith in you, and for anyone who has never encountered you in a way that allowed them to embrace you. We beg your forgiveness for anything we have ever done that has prevented someone from knowing and loving you.

Mary, teach us to believe in your son, and to trust that he always acts with our best interests in mind.

Amen.

. . . .

The Second Glorious Mystery

The Ascension

Fruit of the Mystery: Desire for Heaven

Reflection:

Jesus' Enemies

There are two sides to every story. When they dragged Jesus before Pilate, they thought that would be it. When they watched him being scourged, they thought no man could endure and survive it, but he did. When they crowned him with thorns, they mocked him, thinking there could be no retribution.

When he was sent out to Golgotha to carry a cross, they celebrated that their will was being done. When they nailed him to the cross, they thought they were rid of him forever. When he mumbled from the cross, they thought he was a madman. And when he screamed out in the agony a man feels when death is near, they thought they had won.

But what they thought was the end was only the beginning.

When the tomb was empty, they claimed it was fraud. When they learned the truth, they were afraid. When he started appearing to people, their illusion crumbled. When his followers rose up and peacefully told his story wherever people would listen, their fear grew.

When they harassed his followers, they were met with peace, and they were perplexed. When they watched his communities living around love, respect, kindness, compassion, and generosity, they were baffled. And when in the face of death his followers showed hope, not fear, they were intrigued and amazed.

There are two sides to every story. What side of the story are you going to place yourself?

What does it mean to ascend? It means to rise. Christians are called and challenged every day to ascend above situations. The opposite of ascend is descend. The world encourages us to descend into the-worst-version-of-ourselves. But every day we are called to ascend and become the-very-best-version-of-ourselves.

Now, place yourself there with the disciples as Jesus bids them farewell and sends them out to change the world. After forty days of eating and drinking with his disciples, Jesus ascends body and soul into heaven.

Jesus did exactly what he said he would do. He was a man of his word. Why do we ignore and doubt his words so often?

He said he would return one day. Do you ever think about it? Imagine if he came today. Are you ready? Would we recognize him? God's chosen people missed him the first time. Would we miss him the second time?

Prayer:
With these inspirations in our hearts and minds, we turn to you, Jesus, and pray.

Lord, give us the courage to take you at your word, and to take your words seriously. Help us to resist the temptation to water down your words or pretend that they are anything but an invitation to radically change our lives.

Jesus, teach us to ascend beyond mediocrity, laziness, self-deception, procrastination, fear, doubt, instant gratification, self-sabotage, indecision, escapism, self-loathing, pride, and selfishness.

We resolve today, Lord, to listen more carefully to the words of the Gospel, and to try harder than ever before to live them in our lives.

Jesus, we offer this decade to you for our homeland and the people of that land. Bless our homeland with faith and values that help everyone in society to ascend. We also pray in a special way for anyone who is living in a country other than the country of their birth, especially those who have been forced to relocate against their will. Liberate all men and women, in all countries, from prejudice against the immigrant and stranger. Remind us that we are all immigrants on this earth, just passing through, pilgrims on our way to our true home with you in heaven.

Mary, please pray that we can let go of any petty prejudices that we allow to rule our hearts, minds, and lives.

Amen.

The Third Glorious Mystery

Pentecost

Fruit of the Mystery: Friendship with the Holy Spirit

Reflection:

What Are You Afraid Of?

The disciples were afraid. Most of us have probably never experienced fear like the fear that gripped them. They were afraid for their lives—afraid the mob would kill them, yes, but also afraid of what was next for them. What would they do now that Jesus was gone?

Then the Holy Spirit descended upon them and transformed them. Their fear was banished, and they were filled with courage. This is the greatest before-and-after sequence the world has ever seen.

Imagine yourself there, in the Upper Room. There is an eerie silence. The fear is palpable. Then the wind begins to blow and the shutters on the windows rattle, and the wind keeps growing until it is howling, and now the shutters are shaking so violently that you sense at any moment they will be ripped from their hinges and fly off into the night. But then an incredible peace descends upon the room and fills the disciples, reminding them of the peace they felt the first day they agreed to follow Jesus. You feel this deep peace too, and you want to hold on to it so it never ends. But then the disciples begin to stir; they get up, filled with a new sense of urgency. The contrast is blinding. A few minutes ago they were paralyzed by fear; now they are animated with a boldness and courage you have never seen before. They begin to leave the Upper Room, and you are left sitting there. Should you go with them? Should you stay put? Should you go back to your ordinary life and pretend you never experienced what you just experienced?

We all need what I like to call a Pentecost Moment, that moment when things finally click into place and the genius of Catholicism makes sense to us. For some people it is a book; for others it is a retreat such as Welcome, or a pilgrimage. There are millions of baptized Catholics and non-Catholic Christians who have not yet experienced their Pentecost Moment. You and I are called and chosen to collaborate with God and help facilitate them.

But our transformation doesn't occur in a single moment. That is just the beginning, the jolt that gets us to see that we are sleepwalking through life and awakens us to all the possibilities.

Now we need daily conversion to chase the selfishness from our hearts, minds, bodies, and souls. But we resist this ongoing transformation into the-very-best-version-of-ourselves. We resist the very things that will make us happy. This is the great paradox of our lives.

Why won't we surrender once and for all to God and allow him to do powerful things in us and through us? What are we afraid of?

Prayer:
With these inspirations in our hearts and minds, we turn to you, Jesus, and pray.

Jesus, send the Holy Spirit upon us again today. Liberate us from our fears and give us the courage to make ourselves 100 percent available to you.

Raise up more ministries and disciples dedicated to creating Pentecost Moments for men, women, and children who have never had a chance to really know your dreams for their lives. Remove from us the false contentment that makes us comfortable with maintenance and mediocrity. Give us a hunger for mission. Open our eyes to see all the people around us who are drowning spiritually, and give us the courage to throw them a lifeline.

Jesus, we offer this decade of the Rosary as a prayer begging you to unleash a new Pentecost in the lives of millions of people. We pray for anyone who will encounter a Pentecost Moment today. Give them a vision of how much better their lives will be if they follow you, and give them the courage to embrace this opportunity. We also ask you to renew our commitment to mission. Finally, we pray in a very special way for anyone who has had his or her image of God corrupted. Heal them so they can discover your love and providence like never before.

Mary, please pray for us that we will learn to hear God's voice in our lives more clearly with every passing day, and teach us to become great friends with the Holy Spirit.

Amen.

The Fourth Glorious Mystery

The Assumption

Fruit of the Mystery: Aging and Dying Gracefully

Reflection:

The Next Life

There is another reality we know almost nothing about. What is heaven like? People have been speculating for thousands of years, yet in truth nobody knows. But it is good for us from time to time to think about what it might be like, and at the same time to be ever mindful that it is infinitely better than we can even imagine. St. Paul reminds us, "No eye has seen, no ear has heard, and no heart can conceive, what God has prepared for those who love him" (1 Corinthians 2:9). Heaven is more beautiful than the most beautiful thing you have ever seen. It is more beautiful than the most beautiful thing you have ever heard. We are simply incapable of conceiving how amazing heaven is.

One of the greatest spiritual dangers is intellectual pride. It is so easy to fall into the trap of thinking we know a lot, when in reality even those among us who know the most know very little. What we don't know about God dwarfs what we do know about God. And when it comes to the afterlife, we know even less.

Pride, arrogance, and ego can all play large roles in our lives and become huge obstacles that prevent us from hearing God's voice clearly. But in Mary we find the antidote for all three: humility.

Mary's radical humility is an encyclopedia of lessons about the inner life. Imagine how rich her inner life must have been. Imagine what it was like for the first Christians to seek her counsel and guidance. Then, at the end of her life, Mary was taken body and soul into heaven, her reward for a life lived entirely for God.

What's keeping you from just giving everything to God? It's hard to do when you are still in love with your sins, when you are obsessed with what other people think about you, when you like to be the one in control. Are you ready to surrender once and for all to God? How would your life be different if you did?

Prayer:
With these inspirations in our hearts and minds, we turn to you, Jesus, and pray.

Lord, fill us with a desire for heaven. Help us to want to be with you more than anything this world has to offer. And give us the grace and courage to strive for heroic virtue, become the-best-version-of-ourselves, and live holy lives.

Jesus, we offer this decade to you for all those people who have never had the joy and privilege of knowing you and your mother. We pray in a special way for the men and women of other religions; inspire them to rigorously seek truth and never be afraid of where it might lead them.

Mary, remind us that we are pilgrims passing through this world, and teach us to age and die gracefully.

Amen.

The Fifth Glorious Mystery

The Crowning of Mary Queen of Heaven

Fruit of the Mystery: True Devotion to Mary

Reflection:

Context is Beautiful

The glory of this world fades, and fades quickly. And yet so often we chase the glory of this fleeting world with reckless abandon. Many men and women will do anything to accomplish glory in this world. Jesus invites us to seek eternal glory with the same energy and zeal. Are you more passionate and enthusiastic about the things of this world or the things of the next world? Are you more passionate about accumulating things in this world than about caring for the less fortunate, relieving the suffering of the poor, and working to eradicate injustice?

God invites us to look at everything in the context of eternity. Context is a beautiful thing, because it shows us the true value of things. A billionaire cares little about his money if his five-year-old son has cancer. That's context. When the doctor tells you that you have only six months to live, you very quickly develop clarity around what matters most and what matters least. That's context.

Context gives us the clarity we need to make great decisions.

The presence of Jesus in her life allowed Mary to constantly see things in the context of love and eternity. If we ask her to accompany us in our journey, she will share this perspective with us, and we will discover the true value of things.

Unless we allow love to rearrange our priorities, when death comes to us, as it comes to us all eventually, our hearts will be filled with regret . . . and that is a horrible way to die.

Mary, your courage, fidelity, and humility greatly pleased the Father, Son, and the Holy Spirit, and now they crown you Queen of Heaven. Mother of God, no greater title exists on earth, as no greater creature than you existed. Queen of Heaven: Other than God, no greater title exists in heaven.

This Mary, who is your spiritual mother and mine, is the most celebrated woman on earth and in heaven. Who is greater than Mary? None but God.

Prayer:

With these inspirations in our hearts and minds, we turn to you, Jesus, and pray.

Lord, open the eyes of my soul a little more each day so I can see things as they really are. Rearrange my priorities around love of God and love of neighbor. Put everything in my life in the context of gospel values and eternity so I can see the true value of things.

Jesus, I offer you this decade in gratitude for this day and all the blessings you have filled my life with. Forgive me for the times I have dwelled in my selfishness and been ungrateful. I am especially grateful for the gift of faith and the grace to pray this Rosary today. Who knows where I would be and what I would be doing without your gentle and persistent call to live a life of virtue?

Mary, thank you for this opportunity to pray with you. Wrap me in your mantle, wrap my family and friends in your mantle, wrap all of humanity in the protection of your mantle.

Amen.

The Stations of the Cross

First Station

Jesus is Condemned to Death by Pilate

V: We adore You, O Christ, and we bless you.
R: Because by Your Holy Cross, You have redeemed the world.

V: Who is this person condemned to death?
"If there is one person we should each get to know it is Jesus– the carpenter from Nazareth, the itinerant preacher, the Son of God, the King of kings and Lord of lords, the Lamb of God, the new Adam, the Messiah, the Alpha and the Omega, the chosen one, the light of the world, the God-man who wants good things for us more than we want them for ourselves, the healer of our souls."
- *Rediscover Jesus*

R: O my God,
I firmly believe that You are one God
in three Divine Persons,
the Father, Son and Holy Spirit.
I believe that Your Divine Son
became man and died for our sins,
and that He will come to judge
the living and the dead.
I believe these and all the truths,
which the Holy Catholic Church teaches,
because You have revealed them,
Who can neither deceive nor be deceived.
Amen.

- *The Act of Faith*

All: My Lord and my God,
I firmly believe in You.
Take the blindness from my eyes,
so that I can see all people and things as you see them.
Take the deafness from my ears,
so that I can hear your truth and follow it.
Take the hardness from my heart,
so that I can live and love generously.
Give me the grace to allow You
to transform me a little more each day
into the person you created me to be.
Amen.

- *Teach Lead Serve*

Second Station

Jesus Takes Up His Cross

V: We adore You, O Christ, and we bless You.
R: Because by Your Holy Cross You have redeemed the world.

V: Jesus came to earth to take up His cross and save us. "Saint Teresa of Avila tells us: 'Remember you have only one soul; that you have only one death to die; that you have only one life, which is short and has to be lived by you alone; and there is only one glory, which is eternal. If you do this, there will be a great many things about which you care nothing.'"
- *The Book of Courage*

R: Jesus Christ tells us:
"If anyone wishes to come after Me,
he must deny himself and take up his cross daily
and follow Me.
For whoever wishes to save his life
will lose it,
but whoever loses his life for My sake
will save it.
What profit is there
for one to gain the whole world
yet lose or forfeit himself?
Whoever is ashamed of Me and My words,
the Son of Man will be ashamed of
when He comes in His glory
and in the glory of the Father and of the holy angels."
- *Luke 9:23-26*

All: The world is incredible in many ways.
But in lots of other ways, it is a mess,
and the mess causes a lot of suffering for a lot of people.
There is a universal sense that all is not well,
and that the world needs changing.
The mess manifests in lots of ways:
Poverty. Starvation. Hatred. Pollution.
Greed. Crime. War. Human trafficking.
Divorce. Violence. Lying. Cheating.
Stealing. Prejudice. Sexual abuse.
Conflict. Unemployment. Loneliness.
- *Decision Point*

Third Station

Jesus Falls the First Time

V: We adore You, O Christ, and we bless You.
R: Because by Your Holy Cross You have redeemed the world.

V: Jesus did not let a falling become a failure. Jesus got up and continued.
"Now is the time to start thinking about how I can make a difference. Now is the perfect time to start thinking or rethinking about my mission in life. My first step is just to recognize that most of the mess—and most of the suffering—in this world is caused by sin. When we reject God's plan and pursue our own selfish agenda we leave behind us a trail of heartache and suffering. Sin makes us unhappy, and it brings misery to others .... But the more I align myself with God, the less mess, heartache and suffering I cause."
- Decision Point

R: God has created me to do him some definite service:
He has committed some work to me
which He has not committed to another.
I have my mission—
I may never know it in this life,
but I shall be told it in the next.

I am a link in the chain,
a bond of connection between persons.
He has not created me for naught.
I shall do His work.
I shall do good.
I shall be an angel of peace,
a preacher of truth in my own place,
while not intending it—if I do but keep his Commandments.
Therefore I shall trust him.
Whatever, wherever I am I can never be thrown away.
If I am in sickness, my sickness may serve him;
in perplexity, my perplexity may serve him;
if I am in sorrow, my sorrow may serve him.
He does nothing in vain.
He knows what he is about.
He may take away my friends.
He may throw me among strangers,
He may make me feel desolate,
make my spirits sink,
hide my future from me—
still He knows what He is about.
- *John Henry Cardinal Newman*

All: O God,
grant us in all of our duties, Your help;
in all of our perplexities, Your guidance;
in all our dangers, Your protection;
And in all our sorrows, Your peace.
- *St. Augustine*

Fourth Station

Jesus Meets His Mother Mary

V: We adore You, O Christ, and we bless you.
R: Because by Your Holy Cross You have redeem the world

V: Our life journey is To Jesus through Mother Mary.

Saint Mother Teresa of Calcutta recalls:
"A gentlemen of the Protestant faith, the son-in-law of Malcolm Muggeridge, told me, 'I love you, your work, everything I see, but there is one thing I do not understand: Our Lady, you are full of Mary."

I replied to him: "No Mary, No Jesus—no mother, no son." A few months later he sent me a card with these words printed in big letters: "I believe, no Mary, no Jesus! This has changed my life."
- *Do Something Beautiful for God*

R. The Angel of the Lord declared unto Mary;
and she conceived of the Holy Spirit.
Behold the Handmaid of the Lord . . .
be it done unto me according to your word.
The Word became flesh . . .
and dwelt among us.

Let us pray:
Pour forth, we beseech thee,
thy grace into our hearts,
that we, to whom the Incarnation of Christ, your Son,
was made known by the message of an Angel,
might, through His passion and cross,
be brought to the glory of the resurrection.
Through the same Christ, our Lord.
Amen.

All: Hail Mary, full of grace,
the Lord is with thee.
Blessed art thou amongst women,
and blessed is the fruit of thy womb, Jesus.
Holy Mary, Mother of God,
pray for us sinners,
now and at the hour of our death.
Amen.

Fifth Station

Simon of Cyrene Helps *Jesus* Carry His Cross

V: We adore You, O Christ, and we bless You.
R: Because by Your Holy Cross You have redeemed the world.

V: God has given each one of us a portion of the Divine Plan to perform.
"For thousands of years God has been using ordinary people to do extraordinary things. God delights in dynamic collaboration with humanity. God doesn't necessarily choose the people who are best educated or those who are good-looking; God doesn't choose people because they are in positions of power and authority; and God doesn't always choose the most eloquent and persuasive. There is one type of person that God has used powerfully over and over again throughout history. It is the prerequisite for mission. God does incredible things with the people who make themselves available to Him."
- Decision Point

R: Our mission as Catholics is not merely to move through the world, leaving it unchanged. Changing the world is part of our mission . . . . But we need to focus first and foremost on becoming men and women of virtue and character, and leading others to do the same.

Every good thing we hope for the world will flow from the reemergence of character and virtue in our lives in society . . . . We believe that Jesus offers us the best way to live. We want to share that best way with others. And that is Evangelization—Helping others to discover the love of God and the wisdom of His ways; helping people to live with their best possible life and become the best version of themselves, helping people to discover the best way to live.This Evangelization is the ultimate form of love of neighbor.
- *The Four Signs of A Dynamic Catholic*

All: Come, Holy Spirit,
I invite you into the very depths of my being.
Lead me, guide me, coach me,
encourage me, and challenge me.
Direct me in all things.
Teach me to become a great decision maker,
so that in every moment of every day
I can choose what is good, right, noble, and just.
Amen.
- *Decision Point*

Sixth Station

Veronica Wipes The Face of *Jesus*

V: We adore You, O Christ, and we bless You.
R: Because by Your Holy Cross You have redeemed the world.

V: God motivates each of us to do our part, small or grand. "It is not the critic that counts; nor the man who points out how the strong man stumbled or where the doer of deeds could have done them better. The credit belongs to the man who is actually in the arena; whose face is marred by dust and sweat and blood; who strives valiantly; who errs, and comes short again and again, because there is no effort without error and shortcomings, who does actually try to do the deed; who knows the great enthusiasm, the great devotion, and spends himself in a worthy cause; who, at worst, if he fails, at least fails well daring greatly. Far better it is to dare mighty things, to win glorious triumphs even though checkered by failure, than to rank among those timid souls who neither enjoy nor suffer much, because they live in the gray twilight that knows neither victory nor defeat."
- Theodore Roosevelt

R. "When asked 'Which is the greatest of the commandments?' With clarity and power, and genius of simplicity, Jesus perfectly summarizes the Gospel.

This was Jesus' response:
'You shall love the Lord your God with all your heart, with all your soul, and with all your mind.' This is the greatest and first commandment. And the second is like it: 'You shall love your neighbor as yourself.' (Matthew 22:39) In forty words Jesus gives us a mini-Gospel." Look how Veronica fulfilled these two commandments in one simple gesture by just wiping the face of a condemned Man.
- *Rediscover Jesus*

All: Grant me, O Lord my God,
a mind to know you,
heart to seek You,
wisdom to find You,
conduct pleasing to You,
faithful perseverance in waiting for You,
and a hope of finally embracing You.
Amen.
- *St. Thomas Aquinas*

Jesus Falls the Second Time

V: We adore You, O Christ, and we bless You.
R: Because by Your Holy Cross You have redeemed the world.

V: Once our heart is firmly set on a true goal, nothing can stop us. God never goes back; God always moves forward. Adam and Eve were banished from the garden. God could have redeemed them and sent them back to the garden, but God didn't. God had two reasons: God always wants our future to be bigger than our past, and God always moves forward.

R: So, God, let us press on towards the future
that You have envisioned for us and for our Church.
It is time for us to become a people of possibility again.
Too much of what we do
is governed by a very limited way of thinking.
We gravitate toward what is manageable,
rather than imagining what is possible.
We have lost touch with best practices
and settle for the way things have always been done.
Now is the time for us
to reimagine what incredible things are possible
if we walk with You, God.

Now is the time for us Catholics
to become a people of possibility.

All: Now is the time we all need
to rediscover Catholicism.
We can try to rediscover it every day.
When we seek in earnest to rediscover Catholicism
we will never be disappointed.
Help us to set our egos and personal agendas aside.
Catholicism is old.
But if we had an ancient treasure map,
we would not throw it away just because it was old.
No.
The age of the map doesn't matter.
What matters is whether or not it leads to treasure.
Catholicism is a treasure map.
It may be old but it still leads us to treasure.
Help us pick up our cross and follow the treasure.
Amen.

- *Rediscover Catholicism*

Eighth Station

Jesus Meets the Women of Jerusalem

V: We adore you, O Christ, and we bless You.
R: Because by Your Holy Cross You have redeemed the world.

V: So very much of the Work of Redemption is accomplished by holy women.
"Serving others is at the core of the mission
God has for his children.
When it comes to serving people in need,
our family, the Catholic Church,
has an incredible track record.
The Church feeds more people,
houses more people,
clothes more people, educates more people,
and takes care of more sick people
than any other institution in the world.
And the Church achieves this
through the action of ordinary Catholics
like you and me."
Probably these women of Jerusalem did much the same in their day.
- *Beautiful Mercy*

R: The Church's first truth
is the love of Christ.
The Church makes herself a servant of this love
and mediates it to all people:
a love that forgives
and expresses itself in the gift of oneself.
Consequently, wherever the Church is present,
the mercy of the Father must be evident.
In our parishes, communities, associations and movements,
in a word,
wherever there are Christians,
everyone should find an oasis of mercy.
- *Pope Francis*

All: I expect to pass through this world but once;
Any good thing therefore that I can do,
Or any kindness that I can show
To any fellow creature,
Let me do it now;
Let me not defer or neglect it,
For I shall not pass this way again.
- *Stephan Grellet*

Jesus Falls the Third Time

V: We adore You, O Christ, and we bless You.
R: Because by Your Holy Cross You have redeemed the world.

V: Jesus' third fall relates to so many innocent people who are trapped in the cycle of disadvantage.

"Weeping for other people's pain does not only mean sharing in their sufferings, but also above all realizing that our own actions are a cause of injustice and inequality."
- Pope Francis

R: On Jesus' day of humiliation, He was brought before Pilate, taken by the guards, flogged, given a crown of thorns, mocked, hit in the face, and forced to carry His own cross. They scourged His body, ripping the flesh open and inflicting nearly unbearable pain. Yet Jesus endured it . . . . Jesus's entire mission is forgiveness. That is because God's plan for the whole world is forgiveness and reconciliation. In a word, that is God's heart: forgiveness . . . . The more you forgive, the more you will be forgiven. That is a basic law of the harvest and of the kingdom of God (Galatians 6:7-8). Do you want love? Then give love away. You want to receive peace? Give peace away. Do you want forgiveness? Know that the more you forgive, more forgiveness you will receive.
- Everybody Needs to Forgive Somebody

All: Then Peter came up and said to [Jesus],
Lord, how often shall my brother sin against me,
and I forgive him?
As many as seven times?
Jesus said to him,
"I do not say to you seven times,
but seventy times seven.
Therefore the kingdom
may be compared to a king
who wished to settle accounts
with his servants.
When he began the reckoning,
one was brought to him
who owed him ten thousand talents;
and as he could not pay,
his lord ordered him to be sold,
with his wife and children
and all that he had,
and payment to be made.
So the servant fell on his knees,
imploring him,
'Lord, have patience with me,
and I will pay you everything.'
And out of pity for him
The lord of that servant released him
And forgave him the debt."
- *Matthew 18:21-27*

Tenth Station

Jesus Is Stripped of His Clothing

V: We adore You, O Christ, and we bless You.
R: Because by Your Holy Cross You have redeemed the world.

V: Naked we came into this world, and, willingly or not, naked we will go out of this world.
We are not called to give begrudgingly. It is not even a willingness to do good that God calls us to. Far above these, when we are at our best as human beings, we are filled with an eagerness to do good, an eagerness to give generously, and an eagerness to help our brothers and sisters regardless of what ocean or idea separates us. "May God bless us all with an eagerness to live generously."
- The Four Signs of a Dynamic Catholic

R: The greater the sacrifice of oneself,
of one's own inclinations,
of one's own intelligence,
of one's own preferences because of obedience,
that much greater is the love shown towards God.
- *St. Maximilian Kolbe*

All: Lord, take all my freedom.
Accept my memory,
my understanding, and my will.
You have given me a call that I have and hold dear.
I return it to You, that it may be governed by Your will.
Give me only Your grace and the gift of loving You,
And I will be rich enough;
I will ask for nothing more. Amen.
- *St. Ignatius Loyola*

Jesus Is Nailed To The Cross

V: We adore You, O Christ, and we bless You.
R: Because by Your Holy Cross You have redeemed the world.

V: We admire people who are joyful in spite of many difficult circumstances.
"Pardon is the instrument placed into our fragile hands to attain serenity of heart. To let go of anger, wrath, violence, and revenge are necessary conditions to living joyfully."
- *Pope Francis*

R: "[Some of the poorest of the poor are nailed permanently to a cross.] The deterioration of the environment and of society affects the most vulnerable people on the planet: 'Both everyday experience and scientific research show that the gravest effects of all attacks on the environment are suffered by the poorest.' . . . . Today, we have to . . . hear both the cry of the earth and the cry of the poor."
- *Pope Francis*

All: Lord, make me an instrument of your peace;
where there is hatred, let me sow love;
where there is injury, pardon;
where there is error, truth;
where there is doubt, faith;
where there is despair, hope;
where there is darkness, light;
and where there is sadness, joy.

O Divine Master,
grant that I may not so much seek to be consoled
as to console;
To be understood as to understand;
to be loved as to love.
For it is in giving that we receive;
It is in pardoning that we are pardoned;
And it is in dying that we are born to eternal life.
Amen.
- *St. Francis of Assisi*

Twelfth Station

Jesus Dies On The Cross

V: We adore You, O Christ, and we bless You.
R: Because by Your Holy Cross You have redeemed the world.

V: John's Gospel shows Jesus dying like no other: rather He handed over His own spirit.
"God does not die on the day when our lives cease to believe in a personal deity, but we die on the day when our lives cease to be illumined by the steady radiance, renewed daily of a wonder, the source of which is beyond all reason."
- *Dag Hammarskjold*

R: Jesus, You died for me,
to forgive my sins.
Help me to live a worthy life
so I can be one with you in paradise.
Help me to forgive all others so I can say sincerely,
"Father forgive them,
for they do not know what they do."
Help me wish well of all others and say without guile:
"Truly, today you will be with me in paradise."
Help me treat all others as loving family, saying:
"Woman, this is your son;

Friend, this is your mother."
Help me at my last hour to trust You,
even though I may feel like saying:
"My God, my God, why have you forsaken me?"
Help me to seek first Your Kingdom in this world
so I can say finally: "I thirst: for truth and freedom,
for peace and justice."
Help me to fulfill my life's purpose,
so that I can say with You:
"It is finished."
And long before my final hour help me to confess:
"Father, into Your hands I commend my spirit."

All: Lord, teach me to be generous.
Teach me to serve you as you deserve;
to give and not to count the cost,
to fight and not to heed the wounds,
to toil and not seek for rest,
to labor and not to ask for reward,
save that of knowing that I do your will.
Amen.
- *St. Ignatius of Loyola*

Thirteenth Station

Jesus Is Taken Down From The Cross

V: We adore You, O Christ, and we bless You.
R: Because by Your Holy Cross You have redeemed the world.

V: We are all called to help people off their crosses.
"[Mother Teresa,] The tiny, frail nun from Calcutta spoke powerful words in defense of the unborn. She said, 'At our children's home in Calcutta alone, we have saved over three thousand children from abortion. These children have brought so much love and joy to their adoptive parents and have grown up so full of love and joy. Please don't kill the child. I want the child. I am willing to accept any child who would be aborted and give him or her to a married couple who would love the child and be loved by the child.'"
- St. Mother Teresa

R: Look down upon me,
O good and sweetest Jesus,
while before your face I humbly kneel.
Most fervently I pray and beg You
to fix deep within my heart
lively sentiments of faith, hope, and charity,

true sorrow for my sins,
and a firm purpose of amendment.
With deep affection and sorrow
I contemplate your five wounds.
I have before my eyes, O good Jesus,
what David the prophet spoke of You,
as though you were saying it to yourself:
They have pierced my hands in my feet,
They have numbered all my bones.
- *Prayer to Jesus Christ Crucified*

All: God, grant me the serenity
to accept the things I cannot change,
courage to change the things I can,
and wisdom to know the difference.
Living one day at a time,
enjoying one moment at a time,
accepting hardships as a pathway to peace,
taking, as Jesus did, this sinful world as it is,
not as I would have it,
trusting that You will make all things right,
if I surrender to Your will,
so that I may be reasonably happy in this life,
and supremely happy with you forever in the next.
Amen.
- *Prayer of Serenity*

Fourteenth Station

Jesus Is Buried In The Tomb

V: We adore You, O Christ, and we bless You.
R: Because by Your Holy Cross You have redeemed the world.

V: Before He was buried in a tomb, Jesus gave up His Spirit and said "It is finished." Not every person even gets started in life, and not every person receives a proper burial. Mother Teresa pricked the consciences of the 1994 National Prayer Breakfast attendees when she said:

"And if we accept that a mother can kill even her own child, how can we tell other people not to kill one another? How do we persuade a woman not to have an abortion? As always, we must persuade her with love and we remind ourselves that love means to be willing to give until it hurts. Jesus gave even His life to love us. So, the mother who is thinking of abortion, should be helped to love . . . the father is told that he does not have to take any responsibility at all for the child he has brought into the world. The father is likely to put other women into the same trouble. So abortion just leads to more abortion. Any country that accepts abortion is not teaching its people to love, but to use any violence to get what they want. This is why the greatest destroyer of love and peace is abortion."

- *Confessions of a Mega Church Pastor*

R:

All: Christ with me, Christ before me,
Christ behind me, Christ in me,
Christ beneath me, Christ above me,
Christ on my right, Christ on my left,
Christ when I lie down,
Christ when I sit down,
Christ in the heart of every man who thinks of me,
Christ in the mouth of every man who speaks of me,
Christ in the eye that sees me,
Christ in the ear that hears me.

- *St. Patrick*

Jesus Rises From Death

V: We adore You, O Christ, and we bless You.
R: Because by Your Holy Cross, You have redeemed the world.

V: Christ's rising on Easter Sunday is the event that changed the face of history.
"Do not let your life be like a shooting star which lights up the sky for only a brief moment. Let your life be like the sun that always burns brightly in the heavens bringing a light and warmth to all those on earth. Let your light shine!"
- *The Book of Courage*

R: We thank you for this day and for all your blessings.
Help us to remain always grateful
for all You do for us and in us.
watch over in a special way today
anyone who is hungry, lonely, depressed,
addicted, unemployed,
or just in need of human touch
and inspire us to realize
that we are Your partners in the work
You wish to do in the world.

Help us to remain
ever mindful of the great love You have
for each and everyone of us,
and give us the courage to respond
with the bold enthusiasm of a little child.
We ask all this in Jesus' name.
Amen.
- Decision Point

All: Loving Father,
Thank You for this day.
Inspire me to live with passion and purpose.
Help me to discover the genius of Your ways.
Quiet my mind and open my heart
so that I can hear exactly
what You are trying to say to me today.
Give me wisdom to embrace Your ways with joy;
give me courage to walk with You at every moment;
give me strength when the world makes me weary;
and help me to remember that I can always find rest
And renewal in the Scriptures.
Amen.
- Teach Lead Serve

Prayers

The Sign of the Cross

In the name of the Father, and of the Son, and of the Holy Spirit.
Amen.

Our Father

Our Father, who art in heaven, hallowed be Thy name; Thy kingdom come; Thy will be done on earth as it is in heaven. Give us this day our daily bread; and forgive us our trespasses as we forgive those who trespass against us; and lead us not into temptation, but deliver us from evil.
Amen.

Hail Mary

Haily Mary, full of grace. The Lord is with thee. Blessed art thou amongst women, and blessed is the fruit of thy womb, Jesus. Holy Mary, Mother of God, pray for us sinners now and at the hour of our death.
Amen.

Glory Be

Glory be to the Father, and to the Son, and to the Holy Spirit, as it was in the beginning, is now, and ever shall be, world without end.
Amen.

The Apostle's Creed

I believe in God, the Father Almighty, Creator of Heaven and earth; and in Jesus Christ, His only Son, Our Lord, Who was conceived by the Holy Spirit, born of the Virgin Mary, suffered under Pontius Pilate, was crucified, died, and was buried. He descended into Hell.

The third day He arose again from the dead; He ascended into Heaven, sitteth at the right hand of God, the Father Almighty; from thence He shall come to judge the living and the dead. I believe in the Holy Spirit, the holy Catholic Church, the communion of saints, the forgiveness of sins, the resurrection of the body, and life everlasting. Amen.

The Nicene Creed

I believe in one God, the Father almighty, maker of heaven and earth, of all things visible and invisible.
I believe in one Lord Jesus Christ,
the Only Begotten Son of God,
born of the Father before all ages.
God from God, Light from Light,
true God from true God,
begotten, not made, consubstantial with the Father;
through him all things were made.
For us men and for our salvation
he came down from heaven,
and by the Holy Spirit was incarnate of the Virgin Mary,
and became man.
For our sake he was crucified under Pontius Pilate,
he suffered death and was buried,
and rose again on the third day
in accordance with the Scriptures.
He ascended into heaven
and is seated at the right hand of the Father.
He will come again in glory
to judge the living and the dead
and his kingdom will have no end.
I believe in the Holy Spirit, the Lord, the giver of life,
who proceeds from the Father and the Son,
who with the Father and the Son is adored and glorified,
who has spoken through the prophets.
I believe in one, holy, catholic and apostolic Church.
I confess one Baptism for the forgiveness of sins
and I look forward to the resurrection of the dead
and the life of the world to come.
Amen.

Saint Michael Prayer

Saint Michael, the Archangel, defend us in battle. Be our protection against the wickedness and snares of the devil. May God rebuke him, we humbly pray; and do thou, O Prince of the heavenly host, by the power of God cast into hell Satan and all the evil spirits who prowl throughout the world seeking the ruin of souls.
Amen.

Guardian Angel Prayer

Angel of God, my Guardian dear, to whom God's love commits me here, ever this day (or night) be at my side, to light and guard, to rule and guide.
Amen.

The Angelus

V: The Angel of the Lord declared unto Mary.

R: And she conceived by the Holy Spirit. (Hail Mary . . .)

V: Behold the handmaid of the Lord.

R: Be it done unto me according to thy word. (Hail Mary . . .)

V: And the Word was made Flesh.

R: And dwelt among us. (Hail Mary . . .)

V: Pray for us, O Holy Mother of God.

R: That we may be made worthy of the promises of Christ.

Let Us Pray:

Pour forth, we beseech Thee, O Lord, Thy grace into our hearts; that, we to whom the Incarnation of Christ, Thy Son,was made known by the message of an Angel, may by His Passion and Cross, be brought to the glory of His Resurrection through the same Christ our Lord.

Amen.

(The Angelus is customarily prayed at 6 a.m., 12 noon, and 6 p.m.)

Memorare

Remember, O most gracious Virgin Mary, that never was it known that any one who fled to thy protection, implored thy help or sought thy intercession, was left unaided. Inspired by this confidence, we fly unto thee, O Virgin of virgins my Mother; to thee do we come, before thee we stand, sinful and sorrowful; O Mother of the Word Incarnate, despise not our petitions, but in thy mercy hear and answer them.

Amen.

Hail, Holy Queen

Hail, Holy Queen, Mother of mercy, our life, our sweetness and our hope. To thee do we cry, poor banished children of Eve: to thee do we send up our sighs, mourning and weeping in this valley of tears. Turn then, most gracious Advocate, thine eyes of mercy toward us, and after this our exile, show unto us the blessed fruit of thy womb, Jesus. O clement, O loving, O sweet Virgin Mary!

V: Pray for us, O holy Mother of God.
R: That we may be made worthy of the promises of Christ. Amen.

The Magnificat

My soul magnifies the Lord, and my spirit rejoices in God my Savior; Because He has regarded the lowliness of His handmaid; for behold, henceforth all generations shall call me blessed; Because He who is mighty has done great things for me, and Holy is His Name; And His mercy is from generation to generation on those who fear Him. He has shown might with His arm, He has scattered the proud in the conceit of their heart. He has put down the mighty from their thrones, and has exalted the lowly. He has filled the hungry with good things, and the rich he has sent away empty. He has given help to Israel, His servant, mindful of His mercy—Even as He spoke to our father—to Abraham and to his posterity forever.

Morning Offering

Dear Lord, I do not know what will happen to me today. I only know that nothing will happen that was not foreseen by You, and directed to my greater good from all eternity. I adore Your holy and unfathomable plans, and submit to them with all my heart for love of You, the Pope, and the Immaculate Heart of Mary. Amen.

Evening Prayer

Dear Lord, The evening has come and the day is done. Let peace wash over my household throughout the dark of night and in the few still hours of tomorrow morning. Wipe away our troubles. Cleanse us of worry and doubt. Give deep and peaceful rest to our hearts, minds, and souls, so they we may rise in the morning ready to love you and those who cross our paths with great enthusiasm. Amen.

Prayer Before Meals

Bless us, O Lord, and these Thy gifts, which we are about to receive from Thy bounty, through Christ our Lord. Amen.

Prayer Before Meals #2

Father, We thank you for food, friends, and family. We ask you to bless in a special way today the hungry, the lonely, the unemployed, and the discouraged. Bless our friends and families wherever they are today. Inspire them to take the next step in their spiritual journey, whatever that next step might be and however small. And we ask all this through your Son Jesus. Amen.

Anima Christi

Soul of Christ, sanctify me. Body of Christ, save me. Body of Christ, save me. Body of Christ, inebriate me. Water from the side of Christ, wash me. Passion of Christ, strengthen me. O good Jesus, hear me. Within thy wounds hide me. Suffer me not to be separated from thee. From the malicious enemy defend me. In the hour of my death call me and bid me to come unto thee, that with thy saints I may praise thee for ever and ever.
Amen.

Come, Holy Spirit

Come, Holy Spirit, fill the hearts of your faithful and kindle in them the fire of your love. Send forth your Spirit and they shall be created. And You shall renew the face of the earth.

O, God, who by the light of the Holy Spirit, did instruct the hearts of the faithful, grant that by the same Holy Spirit we may be truly wise and ever enjoy His consolations, Through Christ Our Lord,
Amen.

Prayer of Saint Francis of Assisi

Lord, make me an instrument of Your peace. Where there is hatred, let me sow love; where there is injury, pardon; where there is doubt, faith; where there is despair, hope; where there is darkness, light; where there is sadness, joy.

O, Divine Master, grant that I may not so much seek to be consoled as to console; to be understood as to understand; to be loved as to love; For it is in giving that we receive; it is in pardoning that we are pardoned; it is in dying that we are born again to eternal life.
Amen.

Saint Patrick's Breastplate

Christ be with me,
Christ within me,
Christ behind me, Christ before me
Christ beside me, Christ to win me
Christ to comfort me and restore me.
Christ beneath me, Christ above me
Christ in quiet, Christ in danger
Christ in hearts of all that love me
Christ in mouth of friend or stranger.

Prayer for Peace

Lord Jesus Christ, who are called the Prince of Peace, Who are Yourself our peace and reconciliation, Who so often said, "Peace to you," grant us peace Make all men and women witnesses of truth, justice, and brotherly love. Banish from their hearts whatever might endanger peace. Enlighten our rulers that they may guarantee and defend the great gift of peace. May all peoples on the earth become as brothers and sisters. May longed-for peace blossom forth and reign always over us all.
Amen.

The Dynamic Catholic Prayer

Loving Father, I invite you into my life today and make myself available to you. Help me to become the-best-version-of-myself by seeking your will and becoming a living example of your love in the world.

Open my heart to the areas of my life that need to change in order for me to carry out the mission and experience the joy you have imagined for my life. Inspire me to live the Catholic faith in ways that are dynamic and engaging. Show me how to best get involved in the life of my parish. Make our community hungry for best practices and continuous learning. Give me courage when I am afraid, hope when I am discouraged, and clarity in times of decision.

Teach me to enjoy uncertainty and lead your Church to become all you imagined it would be for the people of our times. Amen.

Acts of Faith, Hope, and Love

Act of Faith

O my God,
I firmly believe
that you are one God in three divine Persons,
Father, Son, and Holy Spirit.
I believe that your divine Son became man
and died for our sins and that he will come
to judge the living and the dead.
I believe these and all the truths
which the Holy Catholic Church teaches
because you have revealed them
who are eternal truth and wisdom,
who can neither deceive nor be deceived.
In this faith I intend to live and die.
Amen.

Act of Hope

O Lord God,
I hope by your grace for the pardon
of all my sins
and after life here to gain eternal happiness
because you have promised it
who are infinitely powerful, faithful, kind,
and merciful.
In this hope I intend to live and die.
Amen.

Act of Love

O Lord God,
I love you above all things
and I love my neighbor for your sake
because you are the highest, infinite and perfect good, worthy of all my love.
In this love I intend to live and die.
Amen.

Litany of Mary

Lord, have mercy on us.
Christ, have mercy on us.
Lord, have mercy on us.
Christ, hear us.
Christ, graciously hear us.
God the Father of Heaven,
Have mercy on us.
God the Son, Redeemer of the world,
Have mercy on us.
God the Holy Ghost,
Have mercy on us.
Holy Trinity, one God,
Have mercy on us.
Holy Mary, pray for us.
Holy Mother of God, pray for us.
Holy Virgin of virgins, pray for us.
Mother of Christ, pray for us.
Mother of divine grace, pray for us.
Mother most pure, pray for us.

Mother most chaste, pray for us.
Mother inviolate, pray for us.
Mother undefiled, pray for us.
Mother most amiable, pray for us.
Mother most admirable, pray for us.
Mother of good counsel, pray for us.
Mother of our Creator, pray for us.
Mother of our Savior, pray for us.
Virgin most prudent, pray for us.
Virgin most venerable, pray for us.
Virgin most renowned, pray for us.
Virgin most powerful, pray for us.
Virgin most merciful, pray for us.
Virgin most faithful, pray for us.
Mirror of justice, pray for us.
Seat of wisdom, pray for us.
Cause of our joy, pray for us.
Spiritual vessel, pray for us.
Vessel of honor, pray for us.
Singular vessel of devotion, pray for us.
Mystical rose, pray for us.
Tower of David, pray for us.
Tower of ivory, pray for us.
House of gold, pray for us.
Ark of the Covenant, pray for us.
Gate of Heaven, pray for us.
Morning star, pray for us.
Health of the sick, pray for us.
Refuge of sinners, pray for us.
Comforter of the afflicted, pray for us.

Help of Christians, pray for us.
Queen of angels, pray for us.
Queen of patriarchs, pray for us.
Queen of prophets, pray for us.
Queen of apostles, pray for us.
Queen of martyrs, pray for us.
Queen of confessors, pray for us.
Queen of virgins, pray for us.

Queen of all saints, pray for us.
Queen conceived without Original Sin, pray for us.
Queen assumed into Heaven, pray for us.
Queen of the most holy Rosary, pray for us.
Queen of peace, pray for us.

Lamb of God, who takes away the sins of the world,
Spare us, O Lord.
Lamb of God, who takes away the sins of the world,
Graciously hear us, O Lord.
Lamb of God, who takes away the sins of the world,
Have mercy on us.
Pray for us, O Holy Mother of God,
That we may be made worthy of the promises of Christ.

Grant, we beseech Thee, O Lord God, that we Thy Servants may enjoy perpetual health of mind and body and by the glorious intercession of the Blessed Mary, ever Virgin, be delivered from present sorrow and enjoy eternal happiness. Through Christ Our Lord.

Amen.

Litany of Saint Joseph

Lord, have mercy on us.
Christ, have mercy on us.
Lord, have mercy on us.

Jesus, hear us,
Jesus, graciously hear us.

God the Father of heaven, have mercy on us.
God the Son, Redeemer of the World, have mercy on us.
God the Holy Spirit, have mercy on us.
Holy Trinity, one God, have mercy on us.

Holy Mary, pray for us.
St. Joseph, pray for us.
Renowned offspring of David, pray for us.
Light of Patriarchs, pray for us.
Spouse of the Mother of God, pray for us.
Chaste guardian of the Virgin, pray for us.
Foster father of the Son of God, pray for us.
Diligent protector of Christ, pray for us.
Head of the Holy Family, pray for us.
Joseph most just, pray for us.
Joseph most chaste, pray for us.
Joseph most prudent, pray for us.
Joseph most strong, pray for us.
Joseph most obedient, pray for us.
Joseph most faithful, pray for us.
Mirror of patience, pray for us.

Lover of poverty, pray for us.
Model of artisans, pray for us.
Glory of home life, pray for us.
Guardian of virgins, pray for us.
Pillar of families, pray for us.
Solace of the wretched, pray for us.
Hope of the sick, pray for us.
Patron of the dying, pray for us.
Terror of demons, pray for us.
Protector of Holy Church, pray for us.

Lamb of God, who takes away the sins of the world, spare us, O Jesus.
Lamb of God, who takes away the sins of the world, graciously hear us, O Jesus.
Lamb of God, who takes away the sins of the world, have mercy on us, O Jesus.

He made him the lord of his household
And prince over all his possessions.

Let us pray:
O God, in your ineffable providence you were pleased to choose Blessed Joseph to be the spouse of your most holy Mother; grant, we beg you, that we may be worthy to have him for our intercessor in heaven whom on earth we venerate as our Protector: You who live and reign forever and ever.
Saint Joseph, pray for us.

Chaplet of Divine Mercy

Oh what great graces will grant to souls who say this chaplet; the very depths of My tender mercy are stirred for the sake of those who say the chaplet. Write down these words, My daughter: Speak to the world about My mercy; let all mankind recognize My unfathomable mercy. It is a sign for the end times; after it will come the day of justice. While there is still time, let them have recourse to the fount of My mercy; let them profit from the Blood and Water which gushed forth for them.

- Diary of St. Faustina, 848

Jesus to St. Faustina: "My daughter, encourage souls to say the chaplet which I have given you. It pleases Me to grant everything they ask of Me by saying the chaplet. When hardened sinners say it, I will fill their souls with peace, and the hour of their death will be a happy one."

- Diary of St. Faustina, 1541

"Oh what great graces I will grant to souls who say this chaplet; the very depths of My tender mercy are stirred for the sake of those who say the chaplet. Write down these words, My daughter: Speak to the world about My mercy; let all mankind recognize My unfathomable mercy. It is a sign for the end times; after it will come the day of justice. While there is still time, let them have recourse to the fount of My mercy; let them profit from the Blood and Water which gushed forth for them."

- Diary of St. Faustina, 848

The Chaplet of Mercy is recited using ordinary rosary beads of five decades.

Opening Prayer:

You expired, Jesus, but the source of life gushed forth for souls, and the ocean of mercy opened up for the whole world. O Fount of Life, unfathomable Divine Mercy, envelop the whole world and empty Yourself out upon us.

- Diary of St. Faustina, 1319

O Blood and Water, which gushed forth from the Heart of Jesus as a fount of Mercy for us, I trust in You.

- Diary of St. Faustina, 187

Pray one Our Father, Hail Mary, and Apostles Creed.

On the Large Beads:

Eternal Father, I offer You the Body and Blood, Soul and Divinity of Your dearly beloved Son, Our Lord Jesus Christ/in atonement for our sins and those of the whole world.

On the Small Beads:

For the sake of His sorrowful Passion/have mercy on us and the whole world.

Conclude with:

Holy God, Holy Mighty One, Holy Immortal One, have mercy on us and on the whole world. (3 times)

Let us pray:

Eternal God, in whom mercy is endless and the treasury of compassion inexhaustible, look kindly upon us and

increase Your mercy in us; that in difficult moments we might not despair, nor become despondent, but with great confidence submit ourselves to Your Holy Will, which is Love and Mercy itself. Amen.
- Diary of St. Faustina, 950

Jesus, I trust in You!
Jesus, I trust in You!
Jesus, I trust in You!

Mother of Sorrows, pray for us.
St. Faustina, pray for us.

A Guide to the Sacrament of Reconciliation

Before you make your Confession, use the Examination of Conscience to help you prepare.

Begin your Confession by making the Sign of the Cross.

Then say: Bless me, Father, for I have sinned. It has been (length of time) since my last Confession. (Or: This is my First Reconciliation.) These are my sins: (Tell your sins to the priest.)

After the priest assigns a penance, pray the Act of Contrition: My God, I am sorry for my sins with all my heart. In choosing to do wrong and failing to do good, I have sinned against you whom I should love above all things. I firmly intend, with your help, to do penance, to sin no more, and to avoid whatever leads me to sin. Our Savior Jesus Christ suffered and died for us. In his name, my God, have mercy.

Then the priest prays the Prayer of Forgiveness.

At the end, when the priest blesses you, make the Sign of the Cross with him and say amen.

Examination of Conscience

There are many ways to examine our lives and our consciences. It is healthy to do so from time to time and a pilgrimage provides the perfect oppourtunity to do that. To help you with that process we included here The Beatitudes; some reflections on the Seven Capital Sins; and the Ten Commandments.

Sin is a failure to love God or others by thought, word, deed, or omission. Mortal sin involves grave matter, fully knowing it is evil, and free consent. Venial sin involves a less serious matter.

The Beatitudes

Matthew 5:3-11

Blessed are the poor in spirit,
for theirs is the kingdom of heaven

Blessed are they who mourn,
for they will be comforted.

Blessed are the meek,
for they will inherit the land.

Blessed are they who hunger and thirst for righteousness,
for they will be satisfied.

Blessed are the merciful,
for they will be shown mercy.

Blessed are the clean of heart,
for they will see God.

Blessed are the peacemakers,
for they will be called children of God.

Blessed are they who are persecuted for the sake of righteousness,
for theirs is the kingdom of heaven.

Blessed are you when they insult you and persecute you and utter every kind of evil against you falsely because of me.

The Seven Capital Sins

Pride:

- Ego-vanity, undue self-esteem and admiration.
- Very self-centered, I always have to be number one
- Pushing for my own view/opinion
- Pretending to be who I am not, hypocritical
- God becomes a god to me, and I become the God Covetousness:
- Live to shop and acquire beyond need or reason
- Take and waste, take and waste, take and waste
- Want way beyond my share
- No room left to store more goods

Lust:

- Out-of-control desire for sexual pleasure
- Pre-marital sex, adultery, fornication, prostitution
- Entertaining temptation, and pornography
- Disrespecting, mistreating my spouse
- Masturbation, mutual masturbation, rape

Envy:

- Sadness when another is successful
- Resenting others who are richer, smarter, happier
- Hating, lying, subverting, plotting against
- Criticizing without building up
- Preventing others from advancing

Anger:

- The desire for revenge, to punish
- Road rage, being too sensitive, impatient
- Easily frustrated, short-tempered, short fuse
- Taking stimulants which prompt bad behavior
- Hating, harming, shouting, warring

Gluttony:

- Consuming too much food, drink, meds
- Overweight, due to lack of physical exercise
- Driving when intoxicated
- Depriving others of adequate food, water, health
- Do not set boundaries for conduct

Sloth:

- Unwilling to give due physical or spiritual effort
- Laziness in prayer, work, giving, tithing
- Not witnessing to Christ, not living one's faith
- Not trying to do one's best, settling for mediocrity
- Giving up, avoiding treatment for depression

The Ten Commandments

1. I am the Lord, thy God, thou shalt not have any gods before Me.
2. Thou shalt not take the name of the Lord, thy God, in vain.
3. Remember to keep holy the Sabbath day.
4. Honor thy father and thy mother.
5. Thou shalt not kill.
6. Thou shalt not commit adultery.
7. Thou shalt not steal.
8. Thou shalt not bear false witness against thy neighbor.
9. Thou shalt not covet thy neighbor's wife.
10. Thou shalt not covet thy neighbor's goods.

Prayer for a Safe Journey Home

My holy angel guardian, ask the Lord to bless the journey which I undertake, that it may profit the health of my soul and body; that I may reach its end; and that, returning safe and sound, I may find all at home in good health. Do thou guard, guide, and preserve us.
Amen.

- By Anonymous

Songs

All Creatures of Our God and King

1. All creatures of our God and King
Lift up your voices and with us sing Alleluia, alleluia Thou burning with golden beam Thou silver moon with softer gleam Alleluia, alleluia, alleluia, alleluia, alleluia,

2. Thou rushing wind that art strong Ye clouds that sail in heaven a long Alleluia, alleluia Thou rising morn in praise rejoice Ye light of evening find a voice Alleluia, alleluia, alleluia, alleluia, alleluia,

3. Thou flowing water pure and clear Make music for thy Lord to hear Alleluia, alleluia Thou fire so masterful and bright That gives to man both warmth and light Alleluia, alleluia, alleluia, alleluia, alleluia,

By Francis of Assisi. Words and music in the Public Domain.

Amazing Grace

1. Amazing grace! How sweet the sound that saved a wretch like me! I once was lost, but now am found; was blind, but now I see.

2. "Twas grace that taught my heart to fear, and grace my fears relieved. How precious did that grace appear the hour I first believed.

3. Through many dangers, toils, and snares I have already come. 'Tis grace hath brought me safe thus far and grace will lead me home.

4. The Lord has promised good to me. His Word my hope secures. He will my shield and portion be as long as life endures.

5. When we've been there ten thousand years bright shining as the sun, We've no less days to sing God's praise than when we'd first begun.

6. Amazing grace! How sweet the sound that saved a wretch like me! I once was lost, but now am found; was blind, but now I see.

By John Newton (1779). Words and music in the Public Domain.

Songs

Ave Maria

1. Ave Maria Gratia plena Maria gratia plena Maria gratia plena Ave, ave dominus Dominus tecum Benedicta tu in mulieribus Et benedictus Et benedictus fructus ventris Ventris tui Jesus Ave Maria

2. Ave Maria Mater dei Ora pro nobis pecatoribus Ora, ora pro nobis Ora, ora pro nobis Pecatoribus Nunc et in hora mortis In hora mortis, mortis nostrae In hora mortis nostrae Ave Maria!

Luke 1:29. Latin, 13th C. Words and music in the Public Domain.

Songs

Be Not Afraid

1. You shall cross the barren desert, but you shall not die of thirst. You shall wander far in safety, though you do not know the way. You shall speak your words in foreign lands, and all will understand, You shall see the face of God and live.

(Refrain)

Be not afraid, I go before you always, Come follow Me, And I will give you rest.

2. If you pass through raging waters In the sea, you shall not drown. If you walk amidst the burning flames, you shall not be harmed. If you stand before the pow'r of hell and death is at your side, Know that I am with you, through it all.

(Refrain)

3. Blessed are your poor, for the Kingdom shall be theirs. Blest are you that weep and mourn, for one day you shall laugh. And if wicked men insult and hate you, all because of Me, Blessed, blessed are you!

(Refrain)

Blest Are They

1. Blest are they, the poor in spirit; Theirs is the kingdom of God. Blest are they, full of sorrow; They shall be consoled.

(Refrain)

Rejoice, and be glad! Blessed are you, holy are you! Rejoice and be glad! Yours is the kingdom of God!

2. Blest are they, the lowly ones; They shall inherit the earth. Blest are they, who hunger and thirst; They shall have their fill.

(Refrain)

3. Blest are they, who show mercy; Mercy shall be theirs. Blest are they, the pure of heart; They shall see God!

(Refrain)

4. Blest are they, who seek peace; They are the children of God. Blest are they who suffer in faith; The glory of God is theirs.

(Refrain)

5. Blest are you, who suffer hate All because of me. Rejoice and be glad, yours is the kingdom; Shine for all to see.

(Refrain)

Christ the Lord is Risen Today

1. Christ, the Lord, is risen today, Alleluia!
Sons of men and angels say, Alleluia!
Raise your joys and triumphs high, Alleluia!
Sing, ye heavens, and earth, reply, Alleluia!

2. Love's redeeming work is done, Alleluia!
Fought the fight, the battle won, Alleluia!
Lo! The Sun's eclipse is over, Alleluia!
Lo! He sets in blood no more, Alleluia!

3. Vain the stone, the watch, the seal, Alleluia!
Christ hath burst the gates of hell, Alleluia!
Death in vain forbids His rise, Alleluia!
Christ hath opened paradise, Alleluia!

4. Lives again our glorious King, Alleluia!
Where, O death, is now thy sting? Alleluia!
Once He died our souls to save, Alleluia!
Where thy victory, O grave? Alleluia!

5. Soar we now where Christ hath led, Alleluia!
Following our exalted Head, Alleluia!
Made like Him, like Him we rise, Alleluia!
Ours the cross, the grave, the skies, Alleluia!

6. Hail, the Lord of earth and heaven, Alleluia!
Praise to Thee by both be given, Alleluia!

7. Thee we greet triumphant now, Alleluia!
Hail, the resurrection day, Alleluia!
King of glory, Soul of bliss, Alleluia!
Everlasting life is this, Alleluia!
Thee to know, Thy power to prove, Alleluia!
Thus to sing and thus to love, Alleluia!

8. Hymns of praise then let us sing, Alleluia!
Unto Christ, our heavenly King, Alleluia!
Who endured the cross and grave, Alleluia!
Sinners to redeem and save. Alleluia!

9. But the pains that He endured, Alleluia!
Our salvation have procured, Alleluia!
Now above the sky He's King, Alleluia!
Where the angels ever sing. Alleluia!

10. Jesus Christ is risen today, Alleluia!
Our triumphant holy day, Alleluia!
Who did once upon the cross, Alleluia!
Suffer to redeem our loss. Alleluia!

By Charles Wesley (1739). Words and music in the Public Domain.

For All the Saints

1. For all the saints who from their labors rest,
who thee by faith before the world confessed,
thy name, O Jesus, be forever blest.
Alleluia! Alleluia!

2. Thou wast their rock, their fortress, and their might;
thou, Lord, their captain in the well-fought fight;
thou, in the darkness drear, their one true light.
Alleluia! Alleluia!

3. O may thy soldiers, faithful, true, and bold,
fight as the saints who nobly fought of old,
and win with them the victor's crown of gold.
Alleluia! Alleluia!

4. O blest communion, fellowship divine,
we feebly struggle, they in glory shine;
yet all are one in thee, for all are thine.
Alleluia! Alleluia!

5. And when the fight is fierce, the warfare long,
steals on the ear the distant triumph song,
and hearts are brave again, and arms are strong.
Alleluia! Alleluia!

6. The golden evening brightens in the west;
soon, soon to faithful warrior cometh rest;
sweet is the calm of paradise the blest.
Alleluia! Alleluia!

7. But lo! there breaks a yet more glorious day;
the saints triumphant rise in bright array;
the King of glory passes on his way.
Alleluia! Alleluia!

8. From earth's wide bounds, from ocean's farthest coast,
through gates of pearl streams in the countless host,
singing to Father, Son, and Holy Ghost.
Alleluia! Alleluia!

By William Walsham How (1864). Words and music in the Public Domain.

Songs

Gather Us In

1. Here in this place new light is streaming; Now is the darkness vanished away. See in this space our fears and our dreamings, Brought here to you in the light of this day. Gather us in, the lost and forsaken Gather us in, the blind and the lame; Call to us now, and we shall awaken We shall arise at the sound of our name.

2. We are the young, our lives are a mystery; We are the old, who yearn for Your face. We have been sung throughout all of history, Called to be light to the whole human race. Gather us in, the rich and the haughty Gather us in, the proud and the strong Give us a heart so meek and so lowly Give us the courage to enter the song.

3. Here we will take the wine and the water; Here we will take the bread of new birth. Here you shall call your sons and your daughters, Call us anew to be salt of the earth. Give us to drink the wine of compassion Give us to eat the bread that is You Nourish us well and teach us to fashion Lives that are holy and hearts that are true.

Hail Mary, Gentle Woman

1. Hail Mary, full of grace The Lord is with you Blessed are you among women And blest is the fruit of your womb, Jesus Holy Mary, Mother of God, Pray for us sinners now And at the hour of death. Amen.

(Refrain)

Gentle woman, quiet light, Morning star so strong and bright Gentle mother, peaceful dove Teach us wisdom, teach us love.

2. You were chosen by the Father You were chosen for the Son You were chosen from all women And for woman, shining one.

(Refrain)

Blessed are you among women Bless in turn all women too Blessed they with peaceful spirits Blessed they with gentle hearts

(Refrain)

Songs

Hail, Holy Queen

1. Hail, Holy Queen enthron'd above, O Maria! Hail, Mother of Mercy and of love, O Maria!

(Refrain)

Triumph all ye cherubim, sing with us ye seraphim, Heav'n and earth resound the hymn: Salve, salve, salve Regina!

2. Our life, our sweetness here below, O Maria! Our hope in sorrow and in woe, O Maria!

(Refrain)

3. We honor you for Christ, your Son, O Maria! Who has for us redemption won, O Maria!

(Refrain)

By Contractus Hermannus, adapted by M. Owen Lee, CSB (1930). Words and music in the Public Domain.

Here I Am, Lord

1. I, the Lord of sea and sky, I have heard My people cry. All who dwell in dark and sin My hand will save. I Who made the stars of night, I will make their darkness bright. Who will bear My light to them? Whom shall I send?

(Refrain)

Here I am, Lord. Is it I, Lord? I have heard You calling in the night. I will go, Lord, if You lead me. I will hold Your people in my heart.

2. I, the Lord of snow and rain, I have borne My people's pain. I have wept for love of them. They turn away. I will break their hearts of stone, Give them hearts for love alone. I will speak My Word to them. Whom shall I send?

(Refrain)

3. I the Lord of wind and flame, I will tend the poor and lame. I will set a feast for them. My hand will save. Finest bread I will provide Till their hearts be satisfied. I will give My life to them. Whom shall I send?

(Refrain)

Songs

Holy God, We Praise Thy Name

1. Holy God, we praise Thy name; Lord of all, we bow before Thee! All on earth Thy scepter claim, All in heaven above adore Thee; Infinite Thy vast domain. Everlasting is Thy reign.

2. Hark! the loud celestial hymn Angel choirs above are raising. Cherubim and seraphim, In unceasing chorus praising; Fill the heavens with sweet accord: Holy, holy, holy, Lord.

3. Lo! the apostolic train Join the sacred name to hallow; Prophets swell the loud refrain, And the white-robed martyrs follow; And from morn to set of sun, Through the Church the song goes on.

4. Holy Father, Holy Son, Holy Spirit, three we name Thee; While in essence only One, Undivided God we claim Thee; And adoring bend the knee While we own the mystery.

5. Holy God, we praise Thy Name; Lord of all, we bow before Thee! All on earth Thy scepter claim, All in heaven above adore Thee; Infinite Thy vast domain, Everlasting is Thy reign.

By Ignaz Franz (1774), translated by Clarence Walworth (1853). Words and music in the Public Domain.

Holy, Holy, Holy

1. Holy, holy, holy! Lord God Almighty!
Early in the morning our song shall rise to thee.
Holy, holy, holy! Merciful and mighty!
God in three Persons, blessed Trinity!

2. Holy, holy, holy! All the saints adore thee,
casting down their golden crowns around the glassy sea;
cherubim and seraphim falling down before thee,
who wert, and art, and evermore shalt be.

3. Holy, holy, holy! Though the darkness hide thee,
though the eye of sinful man thy glory may not see,
only thou art holy; there is none beside thee
perfect in pow'r, in love, and purity.

4. Holy, holy, holy! Lord God Almighty!
All thy works shall praise thy name in earth and sky and sea.
Holy, holy, holy! Merciful and mighty!
God in three Persons, blessed Trinity!

By Reginald Heber (1826). Words and music in the Public Domain.

Hosea

1. Come back to Me with all your heart Don't let fear keep us apart. Trees do bend, though straight and tall; So must we to others' call.

(Refrain)

Long have I waited for your coming home to Me And living deeply our new life.

2. The wilderness will lead you To your heart where I will speak Integrity and justice With tenderness you shall know

(Refrain)

3. You shall sleep secure with peace; Faithfulness will be your joy.

(Refrain)

How Great Thou Art

1. O Lord my God, when I in awesome wonder Consider all the worlds Thy Hands have made; I see the stars, I hear the rolling thunder, Thy power throughout the universe displayed.

(Refrain)

Then sings my soul, my Savior God, to Thee, How great Thou art, how great Thou art. Then sings my soul, my Savior God, to Thee, How great Thou art, how great Thou art!

2. When through the woods and forest glades I wander, And hear the birds sing sweetly in the trees, When I look down from lofty mountain grandeur And see the brook, and feel the gentle breeze.

(Refrain)

3. And when I think that God, His Son not sparing, Sent Him to die, I scarce can take it in; That on the Cross, my burden gladly bearing, He bled and died to take away my sin.

(Refrain)

4. When Christ shall come, with shout of acclamation, And take me home, what joy shall fill my heart. Then I shall bow, in humble adoration, And then proclaim: "My God, how great Thou art!"

(Refrain)

I Am the Bread of Life

1. I am the Bread of Life, You who come to Me shall not hunger, And who believe in Me shall not thirst. No one can come to Me Unless the Father beckons.

(Refrain)

And I will raise you up, And I will raise you up, And I will raise you up on the last day.

2. The bread that I will give Is My flesh for the life of the world, And if you eat of this bread You shall live forever, You shall live forever.

(Refrain)

3. Unless you eat Of the flesh of the Son of Man And drink of His blood, And drink of His blood, You shall not have life within you.

(Refrain)

4. I am the Resurrection, I am the Life, If you believe in Me, Even if you die, You shall live forever.
(Refrain)

5. Yes, Lord, I believe That You are the Christ, The Son of God Who has come Into the world.

(Refrain)

Immaculate Mary

1. Immaculate Mary, your praises we sing. You reign now in Heaven with Jesus, our King.

(Refrain) Ave, ave, ave, Maria! Ave, ave, Maria!

2. In Heaven the blessed your glory proclaim. On earth we your children invoke your sweet name.

(Refrain)

3. We pray for our Mother, the Church upon earth, And bless, Holy Mary, the land of our birth.

(Refrain)

By Jeremiah Cummings (1814-1866). Words and music in the Public Domain.

Joyful Joyful We Adore Thee

1. Joyful, joyful we adore thee God of glory, Lord of love Hearts unfold like flowers before thee Opening to the sun above.

2. Melt the clouds of sin and sadness Drive the doubt away Giver of immortal gladness Fill us with the light of day.

3. All thy works with joy surround thee Earth and heaven reflect thy rays Stars and angels sing around thee Center of unbroken praise.

4. Field and and forest, vale and mountain Flowery meadow, flashing sea Chanting bird and flowing fountain Call us to rejoice in thee.

5. Joyful music leads us sunward In the triumph song Joyful music leads us sunward In the triumph song of life.

By Henry Van Dyke (1907). Words and music in the Public Domain.

O God Beyond All Praising

1. O God beyond all praising,
we worship you today
and sing the love amazing
that songs cannot repay;
for we can only wonder
at ev'ry gift you send,
at blessings without number
and mercies without end:
we lift our hearts before you
and wait upon your word,
we honor and adore you,
our great and mighty Lord.

2. The flow'r of earthly splendor
in time must surely die,
its fragile bloom surrender
to you, the Lord Most High;
but hidden from all nature
the eternal seed is sown--
though small in mortal stature,
to heaven's garden grown:
for Christ, your gift from heaven,
from death has set us free,
and we through him are given
the final victory.

3. Then hear, O gracious Savior,
accept the love we bring,
that we who know your favor
may serve you as our King;
and whether our tomorrows
be filled with good or ill,
we'll triumph through our sorrows
and rise to bless you still:
to marvel at your beauty
and glory in your ways,
and make a joyful duty
our sacrifice of praise.

On Eagle's Wings

1. Immaculate Mary, your praises we sing. You reign now in Heaven with Jesus, our King.

You who dwell in the shelter of the Lord, Who abide in His shadow for life, Say to the Lord, "My Refuge, my Rock in Whom I trust."

(Refrain)

And He will raise you up on eagle's wings, Bear you on the breath of dawn, Make you to shine like the sun, And hold you in the palm of His hand.

2. The snare of the fowler will never capture you, And famine will bring you no fear; Under His wings your refuge, His faithfulness your shield.

(Refrain)

3. You need not fear the terror of the night, Nor the arrow that flies by day, Though thousands fall about you, Near you it shall not come.

(Refrain)

4. For to His angels He's given a command, To guard you in all of your ways, Upon their hands they will bear you up, Lest you dash your foot against a stone.

(Refrain)

Songs

One Bread, One Body

(Refrain)

One bread, one body, one Lord of all, One cup of blessing which we bless. And we, though many, throughout the earth, We are one body in this one Lord.

1. Gentile or Jew, Servant or free, Woman or man No more.

(Refrain)

2. Many the gifts, Many the works, One in the Lord Of all.

(Refrain)

3. Grain for the fields, Scattered and grown, Gathered to one For all.

(Refrain)

You Are Mine

1. I will come to you in the silence I will lift you from all your fear You will hear My voice I claim you as My choice Be still, and know I am near.

2. I am hope for all who are hopeless I am eyes for all who long to see In the shadows of the night, I will be your light Come and rest in Me.

(Refrain)

Do not be afraid, I am with you I have called you each by name Come and follow Me I will bring you home I love you and you are Mine.

3. I am strength for all the despairing Healing for the ones who dwell in shame All the blind will see, the lame will all run free And all will know My name.

(Refrain)

Your Notes